HEALING
for Hurting
FAMILIES

God's
HEALING
for Hurting
FAMILIES

*Biblical Principles for Reconciliation
and Recovery*

David L. Thompson
with Gina Thompson Eickhoff

wesleyan
publishing
house

Indianapolis, Indiana

Copyright © 1998, 2004 by Wesleyan Publishing House
All Rights Reserved
Published by Wesleyan Publishing House
Indianapolis, Indiana 46250
Printed in the United States of America

ISBN 0–89827–281–5

Library of Congress Cataloging-in-Publication Data

Thompson, David L. (David Loren), 1940-
  God's healing for hurting families : biblical principles for reconciliation and
  recovery / David L. Thompson with Gina Thompson Eickhoff.
      p. cm.
  Includes bibliographical references.
  ISBN 0-89827-281-5 (pbk.)
  1. Family—Religious life. 2. Problem families. I. Eickhoff, Gina
  Thompson. II. Title.
  BV4526.3.T47 2004
  259'.1—dc22

                                                              2003027842

Previously published by Wesleyan Publishing House as *Holiness for Hurting
People.*

Contents

Preface   Not Just Another Recovery Book   7

Acknowledgements   11

PART 1   **CASE STUDY IN DELUSION**   13

Chapter 1   One Family's Journey Out of Darkness   15

PART 2   **RESOURCES FOR THE JOURNEY**   29

Chapter 2   Holy Love and Human Destiny   31

Chapter 3   Holy Love and Real Life   43

Chapter 4   The Human Connection and Its Problem   55

Chapter 5   Hope for the Human Connection   71

PART 3   **THE DISCIPLESHIP-RECOVERY JOURNEY**   83

Chapter 6   From Delusion to Disclosure   87

Chapter 7   From Destruction to Dynamic   101

Chapter 8   From Parasite to Partner   117

Chapter 9   From Toxic Talk to Constructive
             Communication   135

Chapter 10   From Rage to Reconciliation   153

Chapter 11   From Abandoned Waif to Well-Loved Child   171

Chapter 12   Questions and Reflections   187

Afterword   201

Addendum   The Twelve Steps   205

Notes   207

Works Cited   221

Preface

Not Just Another Recovery Book

Repercussions of Faith, Trivial and Toxic

Christian faith? The church? "Irrelevant at best and toxic at worst" may represent more than media lampooning. It expresses the reluctant opinion of a surprising number of former churchgoers. The amazing capacity of Christian faith to address the major issues of human life has been largely lost on North Americans of the latter twentieth and early twenty-first centuries.

According to studies funded by the Lilly Endowment Inc., most American mainline denominations have become "sideline" bureaucracies. They stand out of touch with the realities of their own members and unable to communicate significant faith to their own children, let alone attract new converts in large numbers. On the other hand, even among groups that have continued to experience growth, too many have left the fold. Their churches simply did not speak to life as they encountered it. In some places sincere quest for spiritual realities only complicated their difficulties and deepened their darkness.

Increasingly, persons seeking spiritual resources for their lives as they actually are have found themselves in one or another of the thousands of "recovery" or so-called "self-help" groups rather than in the church. There they have experienced the support promised but not delivered by the church. There they have discovered a journey of personal, moral, and spiritual transformation. There they have found a journey of "recovery" that should have been the path of Christian salvation and discipleship, and a vision for human relationships that should have been the content of Christian holiness. For many, instead, these words of the faith—"salvation," "discipleship," "holiness," and others—smack of copping out. Or they remain the aspiration of isolated saints.

At the same time, "recovery" and "recovery groups" strike many in the church primarily as a place for some people to "celebrate" their plight as victims. Many suspect these persons "in recovery" are simply seeking an excuse to rehearse the tragedies of their childhood, blame others for their own inadequacies, and use pop psychology to evade responsibility. "Recovery" and "self-help" are just aspects of the psychological seduction and the narcissism of our culture, these skeptics would say.

Current literature on matters of biblical exposition and Christian discipleship on the one hand and recovery issues on the other concentrate on both "end zones." The majority of the playing field remains untouched. *God's Healing for Hurting Families* rests on the conviction that great benefit could come from pursuing recovery issues *in the context of Christian discipleship, in tandem with sound Bible exposition.*

Revelation, Christian Discipleship, and Recovery

God's Healing for Hurting Families stands on Ephesians, the New Testament treatise by the Apostle Paul. It is prompted by my own family's rescue through God's grace in a drug and alcohol rehabilitation program. It claims discipleship is "recovery." It also claims recovery at its best is Christian discipleship. It says Paul's understanding of human destiny as holy love here and now encompasses brilliantly the journey of "health and sobriety" treasured by persons in recovery. It shows how the issues of holy love Paul treats cover precisely the key agendas of recovery. *God's Healing for Hurting Families* claims these agendas of holy love have sufficient depth and breadth to drive the project of human spiritual transformation all the way from an opening awareness of the need for God to the culmination of the human journey. It maintains that the good news of Jesus presented in Ephesians offers not only a marvelous vision of human destiny but the spiritual resources by which to reach it. And it will seek to do so from a reading of Ephesians that does not psychologize the Bible but actually rests on legitimate interpretation, probing the implications of issues raised by the writer.

The extensive common ground exposed between recovery and Christian holiness and discipleship sheds light in both directions at once. On the one hand, the radically liberating, profoundly practical energy of Christian holiness and its vision of holy love becomes clearer in light of recovery thought. This could interest persons in recovery who have dismissed Christian faith as relevant to their health and sanity. It also provides guidance for persons who sense the spiritual vacuum in "recovery" without adequate biblical foundation.

On the other hand, the deadly serious and considerably complex nature of these agendas of the holy life becomes more apparent in light of the issues of so-called "adult child" and addiction recovery. This seriousness engages persons in the church who have reduced Christian discipleship to pietistic rules. It asks the ear of those inclined to trivialize the issues of Christian spiritual growth by dismissing these matters as "faults," "weaknesses," or routinely rehearsed "sins of word, thought, and deed."

Beyond Self-Help and Good Feelings to the Good News

Yet another problem of the sidelined church also concerns us here. Its quest to attract secular persons has too often led it to sacrifice its identity—a suicidal move. Exchanging the distinctive power of the good news of Jesus Christ for religious psychobabble and essentially non-Christian responses to human problems has proven singularly ineffective.

So, while this book will talk often of human feelings and of the critical task of finding, owning, and expressing our feelings, it will aim far beyond "feeling good" about ourselves. And while we will emphasize the self-accountability at the heart of "self-help" ideas, we will discover that the good news in Jesus is fundamentally not about our helping ourselves but about being thoroughly transformed by the Spirit of the living God. We will retrieve biblical words like "salvation" and "holiness" and discover the liberating good news they carry.

Acknowledgements

This book attempts to "mine the gold" from my own family's pain. More than anything I have previously written, this comes from the soul of our family as a whole. It offers insights gleaned from our long and difficult journey through a crisis of major proportions. I have attempted as much as possible to confine myself to my story where it seemed germane to share it. But, by the very nature of the case, at numerous important junctures my story proved inextricably bound to the story of others dear to me.

Without the cooperation and interest of my wife Ede and each of the children, Gina, Scott, and Karin, I surely could not have proceeded. Each one has read and responded helpfully to the manuscript as it unfolded. To Ede and her unfailing love I pay particular tribute. Review of some stretches of our journey together is painful for us both. She has never wavered from her conviction that we could "make it" and could come out the better for it all. Wives of lesser love would have given up on me long ago, I am afraid.

Gina's investment has proved particularly critical and useful. She reads as an accomplished writer in her own right and as the one in the family who has probably pushed the recovery process the furthest. Her detailed notes and keen insights have been indispensable to the point of sharing authorial credit and responsibility. Special thanks goes to her.

Donald M. Joy and Harold Burgess, teaching colleagues here at Asbury Theological Seminary, gave helpful feedback to early forms of the work. Carol Streeter's expertise as an acquisitions editor helped shape its pitch. Thanks goes also to the "Unfinished Business" Sunday school class at the Free Methodist Church, Wilmore, Kentucky, who chewed on early versions of much of what finally surfaced here. Their interest largely inspired this work. Aggressive review and encouragement by J. D., Jr. and LeeAnn Abbott have brought numerous improvements to the final manuscript. I also appreciate very much Nathan Birky's help as General Publisher of The Wesleyan Church when this book was originally released and the editorial work done for him by Bobbie Sease, which improved the product in details on almost every page.

None of these friends and family carry responsibility for shortcomings which remain. They all share some credit for whatever benefit *God's Healing for Hurting Families* may bring to readers. I gladly acknowledge my debt to all of them and my joy in working and living with them.

Part One

Case Study in Delusion

I venture to use my own experience and that of my family as a case study to put flesh and blood on matters easily left cerebral. "Our story" is not itself the good news of life in Jesus. But we are a real-life sample of both the painful web of addiction and, at least in some significant ways, also of the potential of recovery by grace. We illustrate so unfortunately well the blindness common in the church, as well as the transforming miracle of growth in grace that counts.

The seriousness, complexity, and tenacity of human fallenness and sin are painfully evident in our descent into darkness. The intergenerational consequences of this sin and fallenness surface repeatedly, revealing in bold relief the need to take into account the legacy of one's family in the discipleship journey. Our experience tellingly demonstrates the difference between the adoption of respectable habits and the creation of truly redemptive human relationships, the difficulties of seeing oneself and of applying what one "knows" to one's own situation, and the importance of the capacity to feel as a key in that appropriation.

So first, a story.

1

One Family's Journey Out of Darkness

A Relatively Healthy Family

"A relatively healthy family," Ede and I chirped in almost identical words that critical evening in October 1989. Bettye Stull, Director of the Family Renewal Center, a drug and alcohol rehabilitation program, had opened our assessment interview with a question about where we thought we were as a family. A week or so before, we had discovered our middle child was using pot. We were there to get help.

Fortunately the Family Renewal staff didn't tell us everything they knew about our family's desperate needs. Instead they offered us help in dealing with Scott's obvious need and enlisted our whole family's cooperation in getting our situation under control. We took them up on the offer and began a journey out of darkness—a journey I had only begun to grasp.

Good Intentions

How could this have happened to us? How could Ede and I have failed to see what was going on between us and in our very own family? As the depth and breadth of our family's crisis became clearer in the ensuing weeks, my amazement and dismay at my profound blindness grew.

Life was not supposed to turn out this way for a professor of biblical literature, zealously serving the Lord at a seminary squarely in the tradition of Christian holiness and perfection in love. Beyond what was "supposed to be" in some romantic sense, I had lived the last thirty years intentionally seeking to construct the kind of marriage and family that would honor the Master and make tragedy of this sort unlikely. How could we have aimed so high and hit so low? What a miscarriage of good intentions! And what a parade of delusion!

Brave Knight Marries Helpless Maiden

Ede and I married in 1962, the day after my graduation from college. We made a classic match: brave young knight in shining armor rescues naive, helpless damsel. I had all the sophistication and urbanity one would expect of a lad raised in "metro" Lyle, Minnesota (population 513), from a butcher's home in a town with all the animosities and bigotries made famous by Garrison Keillor's tales from Lake Wobegon. Our family had moved to the big city (Austin, Minnesota; twelve stop lights!) where my academic achievement and skill on the clarinet presented me with exciting opportunities. Pursuing a call to Christian ministry, I had gone to college in Indiana.

The number one rule in the Thompson family was "Don't say what you really feel, think, or want." This rule, of which our family was completely unaware, was more important than all our other rules. It was more important than our rules to love Jesus, to go to church, to put things back, to pick up your own toys, to not go to "shows"—not even free ones. It even topped our rules to not smoke, drink, or chew.

In early October 1989, when it became clear that my father would not live long, I went home to see him one last time. Among his final words to me were, "I'm so thankful, Son, that our family has always gotten along with each other." By this he meant that, unlike some of our relatives who give each other the cold shoulder for years, we were still speaking to one another. What we didn't say, and surely could not have said that last day we saw each other, was the reason for this "getting along." As a family we talked little of things that really mattered. We seldom discussed what was actually going on in our families or personal lives. Family conversations covered mainly inane topics or concerned themselves with ridiculing the music, clothes, politics, customs, ideas, religion, and ways of people different from the Thompsons.

I married a woman who grew up in a family with the same rule and another of equal force to cement it in place: "Father, like God, is always right! So disagreeing with Father is disagreeing with God Himself!" An only child, Ede had grown up in vintage Wesleyan Methodist parsonages, within a fifty-mile radius of the denominational school where we met in north central Indiana. Her family had roots and continuity. Her grandfather could spin yarns from his living acquaintance with persons who had worked the canals in northern Indiana and seen Chicago when it was little more than a few cabins by the lake. Edith's family ate Sunday dinner, no matter how sparse, on real china with real silver, napkins, and candles!

Nothing in their family was more important than "following the Lord *very carefully*," as her father would often say, emphasizing the last two words. "Following the Lord" included especially avoiding confrontation of any sort and staying completely clear of any appearance of evil. Ede focused on school and perfecting her piano and organ skills. When I first met her she was the accompanist for the college music department. Her piano magic, in fact, brought us together and launched our romance.

But worldly-wise she was not. As a college junior, she lacked basic information about human reproduction. The sexually explicit content of the required reading assigned for her Marriage and Family class so embarrassed her that she was reluctant to check the books out of the library herself. Being the man-about-town that I was, accustomed to solving as many of her problems as I could, *I* agreed to check out the books for her. It made sense and felt so right! This transaction typified our relationship.

Happily Married Warfare

So we married June 5, 1962, and embarked on the seminary studies in the fall—I in class and she teaching first grade to support us. But surprise of surprises! Being married to a woman who seemed to think, manage, and express her emotions like a child soon proved much less satisfying than one might have guessed from the original romantic fascination with such a person. In fact it proved to be disappointing and disgusting.

It was a still greater surprise to me when Ede finally found words to tell me that being married to a man who treated you like a child was even less fun. Living with someone who wanted to think for you, make your major decisions, tell you what was best for you proved much less satisfying on this side of marriage than it did on the other. Living with a man who said, in effect, what you think and feel and say does not count turned out to be very painful and very frustrating. (It took nearly thirty years for Ede to express this pain and anger directly.)

Early on, battle lines developed over questions about which we both felt strongly, but which we could not come close to expressing clearly or forthrightly. Conversations about matters of consequence seemed to go nowhere. We settled into a routine of "happily married warfare" of increasing seriousness and indirectness. Disagreements regarding our sexual relationship, home maintenance, and the nature of Ede's relationship to my work simmered unresolved.

But our increasing alienation was masked by increased attention to affirmation and affection. The vast majority of the battle was waged *internally*. Though the total time invested in these "discussions" was considerable over the years, I spent relatively little time actually expressing clearly my frustration, disappointment, and anger, or my aspirations, desires, and feelings. I spent huge amounts of time and energy rehearsing like a broken record what I should have said or wanted to say to Ede.

Apparently it was the same for her. Over the first twenty-five years of our marriage she found it nearly impossible to talk in a straightforward manner about features of my behavior she found distressing. She could not find courage to put what she felt and thought and wanted into words. Sounds amazing and impossible, but sadly that's the way it was.

My Heart Walked Out in Despair

Somewhere around 1978 or 1979, I abandoned the field emotionally. I don't remember the exact date, but I recall the night. After one of our fruitless discussions, I walked to the seminary with a deep sense of hopelessness: she would never change. I would not hassle this woman anymore. She could do her thing; I would do mine. I knew *she* had serious personal problems that needed attention. But I despaired of ever seeing her get the help she obviously needed. That *I* had problems as deep or deeper did not occur to me. *She* was the one who needed help.

I would live and let live. I would be the best father I knew how to be to our children. I would love my wife, as those who follow Christ love all persons. I would honor her, care for her, will good for her. But I would quit pretending I felt real husbandly love for her. As for our ridiculous discussions and the endless manipulations involved in trying indirectly to get her to understand my grievances, I was finished. My heart walked out in despair that night. Where this would all lead or how it could all fit together I had no idea.

House projects stopped, without any conscious decision on my part. We had been engaged in remodeling our modified Cape Cod. I had finished the half-story attic, transforming it into three lovely rooms with cathedral ceilings, interesting alcoves for the children and captured storage space everywhere. The final project was my study, made from a postage-stamp-sized porch we enclosed off the living room. The paneling was up, the built-in bookshelves were beautifully stained, varnished, and in place on three walls, and the rug was on the floor. Only the ceiling tile and indirect lighting above the bookshelves remained to be completed. The study stood unfinished for twelve years—the old porch ceiling and lack of lighting mute testimony to my "departure"! Construction on Gina's dollhouse stopped. Work on and planning for landscaping came to a halt. So it went.

Light in the Darkness—Almost

Years before this I had discovered to my utter amazement that my own parents, married already then for decades, were mired in a profound marital crisis. Before that I had not picked up on the several clues to the currents of distrust and anger that moved beneath the surface of our "happy Christian home."

But the most important questions about the entire episode did not occur to me.

- "What might it mean that my family of origin was very different from what I had always understood?"

- "What could it mean that I grew up in a home where the two most important people in my life felt and thought quite differently from what they appeared to think and feel?"

- "How could these dear people, so committed to truth and love, so firmly convinced of the gospel, have lived such a contradiction?"

The fact that these astounding revelations might have tremendous significance for my own life and my own self-understanding did not cross my mind.

I did not think to examine the implications of growing up in a family whose "tree" was dotted on both sides with "colorful" individuals against which a handful of balanced souls stood out in bold relief. Alcoholics, personally and socially dysfunctional people, unfaithful partners, broken marriages, chronically ill, and depressed people held the majority.

That my own family of origin carried essentially the same pathologies as those of my aunts and uncles did not occur to me. The good news about Jesus, which my parents had believed and sought to live since before my birth, this gospel had altered and domesticated my family's pathologies to socially acceptable forms. But it had not changed some essential patterns of behavior or their lethal consequences. The connections did not register.

Saving the World and Losing My Own Soul

By the mid-eighties I was pastoring a Wesleyan church in Rockville, Maryland, five miles outside the D. C. beltway. This church, with which our family had deep and strong personal ties from association during Ph. D. work at The Johns Hopkins

University, had called me in the spring of 1982 with a desperate story. If I could not come, they would have to close the church. Although I was plowing full steam ahead in my work as Associate Professor of Biblical Studies at Asbury Theological Seminary, and enjoying that work immensely, I felt led to "consider" the invitation. It made no sense professionally or financially. But then, when did the demands of the gospel or the leading of the One who carried a cross necessarily make professional or financial sense?

After prayer and reflection, Ede and I decided we should accept the church's call. Since their call and our decision came too late to allow the seminary sufficient time to recruit a replacement, I agreed to delay my resignation until the following year and to teach three courses a semester during the 1982–83 academic year. This would cover my share of our department's load and allow time for a personnel search. We moved our family to D. C. in July 1982 and I spent the next year pastoring and commuting to the seminary in Wilmore, Kentucky—an indispensable man for sure! For the moment too many things were going on to allow for much awareness of family struggles.

When my responsibilities at the church became full-time, seven days a week, old battles at home resurfaced. I was less and less at home—the less the better, so far as I was concerned. The less contact I had with my wife, the less we tangled over agendas we had tracked for years.

Amazingly, the Lord used our fractured family in a wide variety of ways to minister to the Aspen Hill Wesleyan Church and its community. In spite of our imperfect witness and devotion from mixed motives, God called people to Himself and strengthened them in their faith. This represents a tribute to God's grace.

In the spring of 1986 we were preparing to return to Wilmore, where I would resume my post at Asbury Seminary. Walking into our daughter Gina's bathroom a month or so before we were to move, I saw vomit lining the upper part of the stool. To my knowledge no one had been ill or had the flu. In a flash I thought *bulimia!* "Gina's bulimic, for heaven's sake!" I asked Ede if she knew anything about "the remains" in Gina's bathroom. She did. She confided that for some time Gina had been experiencing "eating difficulties." Ede had felt it best not to bother me with this problem! I had so much on my mind with the church and getting ready to move, she felt I wouldn't be able to handle the stress of this problem. Besides, Gina was making progress.

"We've got problems!" was my response. It didn't take a psychiatrist to tell me these symptoms were serious and that they quite likely said something about our family as a whole. With just a few weeks left before we moved, it seemed too late to do anything about it then. I filed it in the "what-in-the-name-of-sense-does-this-mean" box and concentrated on getting us moved to Kentucky. We made the move in July, spent five weeks of quality family time tramping and camping through the western states, and settled back into our house on Asbury Drive. I resumed my teaching. We got the kids back to school and never found reason to pursue Gina's problem.

By January 1988 my heart was so empty, my spiritual life so barren, I cried out to God in utter despair. I found myself wrestling with the theistic question, as I had in the darkest days of my pastoral experience. God—if He existed at all—seemed a million miles from my life. The glib and, to my way of thinking, mindless drivel involved in much of my church's talk about God and His interaction with human beings seemed eminently unsatisfying. But life without God seemed an even more terrible option.

Desperately seeking help, I felt led to ask Deaconess Ann Gulick if she would guide my search for God. This godly and wise woman (missionary, theologian, philosopher, writer, linguist), who had been a student of mine at the seminary ten years earlier and whom I had come to respect deeply, was old enough to be my mother. I had confidence that if anyone could help me, Ms. Gulick could.

At our first meeting I poured out my heart to her, laying before her as clearly as I could my hunger for God and my grave question at times about the validity of the whole faith enterprise. Surprise! She offered no "answer," not even a direct response. Instead she looked straight into my eyes and asked, "At whom are you angry? Against whom do you harbor resentment?" Then she inquired about my prayer and Scripture-reading disciplines, and found them meager. (Of course I spent much time examining Scripture professionally for my work. But I found relatively little time for prayerful reflection upon that Word and appropriation of it for myself.)

Ann set two related agendas for me if I wanted to find God. One, I would find my anger. She correctly perceived that my doubt was not nearly so much a theological problem as it was a personal problem—anger come to rest at the doorstep of God. Second, I would renew the spiritual disciplines in my life: daily Scripture, prayer, and journal. How could one find God apart from the "means of grace"?

At whom are you angry? That's easy! At my wife, that's who, for the same agendas about which I had stewed for over two decades! And at myself and us: for allowing myself to get sidetracked in pastoral ministry; for squandering whatever opportunity I might have had to be a scholar; for allowing myself to come to age forty-eight and still be unable to provide for my family; for allowing us to continue living as though a family can spend two incomes when it only has one; and . . .

Under Ann's direction I set about writing and praying out this anger and offering it to God as best I could, with some "relief" but no substantial change in the structures of our family's interactions.

Though I had no intellectual advances on the questions that brought me to Ann, my willingness to entrust myself to God—whether I ever "felt" Him or not—increased. My perspective on the grace of God active in my "exile" from teaching broadened and became more positive. What to do about the issues that seemed unresolvable with Ede remained a mystery. I saw no way through or around these. The toll these might be taking on our family itself did not compute, in spite of the hours I spent reading, praying, and journaling about the matters.

Connection Reality Crash

As a matter of fact, what was actually happening to our family dangled somewhere beyond my peripheral vision. Ede and I were so locked in a life habit of avoiding reality that I simply could not, or did not, see what was going on. I could not bring myself to face the level of battle going on between my wife and me across a whole array of fronts, and I could not see the pain and struggle of my children starved for authentic love and affirmation. Gina, now in college, was still struggling with food, still beating her body with exercise, still living in continual hyper-stress over grades. Scott, now a senior, was politely and passively but increasingly defiant regarding his antisocial lifestyle, continually truant and openly at odds with the family's values. Karin's most significant friendships and her accelerating flight to an eighth-grade social orbit out of our family's reach bode ill for her future. In other people's families and children, these would have presented obvious signs of deep need.

It must sound utterly implausible. With all the glaring clues I had been given over the years, it would seem the light should have dawned on me. Somewhere along the way I should have seen through the delusion. It did not happen.

It horrifies me to think what would finally have become of our family if Scott's entanglement with drugs had not come to light. Without this reality crash we would surely have perished. Our "relatively healthy" but literally "falling-apart-at-the-seams-family" entered a drug rehabilitation program in which we were given tools and support to stop the lie and to start telling the truth. Our blinders were slowly taken off. We began the process of finding and expressing our feelings, thoughts, perceptions, hurts, and aspirations. We began the process of learning how God's grace could restore and transform our broken connections, and how He could enable our family little by little to put away the lie and talk the truth.

Miracle: Rescue by Holy Love

The Family Renewal Center intervened in our family's plight at several points of need. It provided structure for a family flying apart and running from our chaos and from each other. A schedule of group and individual experiences focused our family's energies around assessing our situation and finding help. Using the Twelve Steps and instruction about family systems and adult children of alcoholics, Family Renewal provided information formally and informally. As we were able, we could see ourselves, our situation, and a way out of the pit—if we would.

The "Twelve Steps," first made famous by Alcoholics Anonymous, provided a loose structure for the group's proceedings. These Twelve Steps, of course, simply order the basic principles of biblical salvation, take them seriously, and candidly apply them to real life. They move from confession of absolute need on through prayer for transformation, promise of restitution, and aspiration to "evangelism." (See Addendum for a complete list of the Twelve Steps.)

Teaching about the disabilities of "adult children"[1] gave us perspective. The "adult child" concept helped all five of us look beneath our present need to the possible causes past and present of our difficulties. It helped us target specific attitudes and behavior for change.

Information about "family systems" helped us see how families live and develop. It presented families as complex, intergenerational ecosystems, subtly and powerfully impacting one another for good or ill, quite apart from intention or plan. We quickly came to see "Scott's problem" as *our* problem. He was one of many symptoms of a family in distress, not just an isolated boy in need. With a blend of intervention, information, support, accountability, and encouragement, the people at Family Renewal put hands and feet and lips on holy love. They became channels of God's saving grace to our family, as did friends in our local church who prayed for and supported us.

Sitting on the floor with other addicts and their families and friends, we shed our aura of respectability and reached out for help. No quick fix, no instantaneous deliverance occurred. But over the course of a year and a half we began to change in profound ways as we entered the "recovery process." We found a process for appropriating God's saving grace to transform our minds and current behavior and to retrieve us from at least some of the consequences of past sin and ignorance.

Ede and I began to learn new patterns of relationship, slowly reversing, at least in some appreciable measure, structures established over years of courtship and marriage. Each of the children found insight and resources to stop their perpetuation of our madness and head in a new direction. As a family we found resolve to face ourselves and act together to live holy love. For us this meant doing what we had never been able to do—confront intolerable behavior in our members young and old, hold ourselves accountable, and face and speak reality. This process of transformed relationships led to a major breakthrough.

Scott, whose problem had led us to the rehabilitation program, "played the game under protest" most of the time and wound up bailing out prematurely. Although he found help in understanding features of our family life, in general his substance abuse and addictive thinking and behavior continued. He spiraled increasingly into a whirlpool with his dream to be lead guitarist in a rock band at the vortex. After working for several months to clarify what was going on—not an easy task when you're working with a con artist—the family finally confronted him with his general refusal to respect the property and person of the rest of the family. We gave him the option of either making a "good faith" resumption of his recovery or finding other living quarters. He chose to move out, inaugurating one of the darkest, loneliest periods of our family's life.

That was April 1992. On June 13 of that summer he participated in his sister Gina's wedding. He ushered at the ceremony and played guitar at both the reception and on a chartered paddleboat ride for the wedding party on the scenic Kentucky River. Over that weekend God pierced his darkness. Three things converged to open his eyes, he said. Family friends from all over the eastern United States came to the wedding, investing time and energy in saying, "We love you and care about your children." These were people Scott knew well, people he knew had been through tough times themselves, people for whom love was more than words. In them he saw the people of God as they are at their best, authentically loving and caring over the long haul. He realized he would never have friends like this.

He saw Gina and Kyle, heard their sincere words of commitment and love, sensed the depth of their commitment and the purity of their love. He knew he would never have a wife like this from the women he now chased.

And he heard the Word of God. In the homily from Ephesians 3:14–21, God actually spoke to him. God used the experiences all together to throw a rope into the pit Scott was digging and set him once again on the road to recovery. His rescue was simply a more dramatic expression of the salvation being worked out gradually in our whole family.

Our family remains needy in many ways. And follow-through for Scott, as for us all, has proved a challenge. We live continually with the temptation to revert to old ways. We stand in need of additional insight and both the continuing grace of God to see ourselves as we are and the continuing power of His Spirit to choose what we know to be His will. But by the grace of God we are no longer trapped in the dark, no longer plunging headlong to destruction. By the grace of God we are by no means perfect, but we are on a very different course. What an amazing miracle of redeeming love!

Brief Insights from the Struggle

The reality crash and subsequent unmasking of our family threw me back utterly and entirely on the grace of God in ways I had never experienced. It knocked out my cockiness and exposed the depth and profundity of the claim of Ephesians 2:8–9. From start to finish, our life and life with God is by His grace! We never were and never will be good enough to save ourselves, and God never had deserted us. He was there all along.

Along with all the good things to be said about our family, and there was much good to be said—our sacrificial ministry, our attempts to be affirming, our generosity and commitment to Christ—we were crippled with vast blindness. Vast delusion laced our lives with lethal sin and deception of which we were scarcely aware.

I found new "life songs" that came to me day in and day out:

> *I need Thee ev'ry hour, most gracious Lord . . .*
> *I need thee; O, I need thee;*
> *Ev'ry hour I need thee . . .*
> (Robert Lowry)

and

> *People* [these people, we Thompson people] *need the*
> *Lord . . .*
> *At the end of broken dreams, He's the open door.*
> *People* [God, I] *need the Lord, people need the Lord,*
> *When will we realize, people need the Lord.*
> (Greg Nelson/Phil McHugh)

Our reality crash and recovery venture opened the depth and breadth of the spiritual journey described in Ephesians 3:18, the journey of grasping, along with all God's people, the astounding extent and implications of the love of Christ. I realized at age fifty I had just barely begun to understand the real-life implications of receiving and living the holy love of Christ. It also reawakened in me the reality and meaning of the word "salvation." This matter of living the destiny God ordained for us, of embarking upon the journey of love, was no mere "enhancement" or "aid to socialization." It was absolute rescue from destruction here and now, quite apart from whatever eternal consequences might be involved. And we actually were being saved, we were changing. It was no dream, but wonderful reality I feared we had squandered for good.

Our situation exposed the range and complexity of the beguilingly simple instructions of Ephesians 4:25–5:2, beginning with these words: "Having put away the lie, let each one speak the truth with his neighbor, for we are related to one another like parts of a body" (AOT).[2] What we were experiencing and learning in our entry to the recovery process dramatically underscored the critical nature of the instruction in these texts. The immensely significant issues—entered through almost every line of apostolic instruction here—captured me as never before and ultimately prompted this project. To this revelation resource we now turn.

Part Two

Resources for the Journey

We may take a short hike with little thought of resources, but backpackers who tackle the Appalachian Trail or the Sierra high country don't set out without adequate resources. Their lives will depend upon them. Discipleship-recovery is a life journey demanding considerable resources. Resources abound for this journey in grace—truth to liberate and direct, people to support and listen, God's Spirit to lead and transform, prayer to strengthen and clarify and connect, roots to ground and orient, and more.

Awareness of those resources seems limited when hurting persons come to the end of themselves. So the resources remain like an oasis over the next sand dune, out of sight and out of reach. Awareness then is key. Information starts to build awareness. Pain and experience move that information to center stage in one's mind.

But critical issues in recovery and discipleship involve not simply ignorance but actual misinformation. Skewed beliefs about oneself, about others, and about God impede and misdirect the journey. They alienate us from the key resources which would be most helpful for the discipleship-recovery trek. So our investigation of the common ground between Christian discipleship and adult child recovery issues must begin with insights that can counter both ignorance and misinformation and provide a place for the whole effort to stand.

Happily, God has already addressed our need for life-directing insight. He has done this by revealing Himself to us. God has disclosed Himself through the world He has made (Rom. 1:19–20; Ps. 19:1–6), through the Word He has given in Holy Scripture (Luke 24:44–46; 2 Tim. 3:15–17), and preeminently through His Son, Jesus of Nazareth (John 1:1–18; Heb. 1:1–4). Since we know God's Son mainly through Scripture, God's revelation in history provides then two primary information resources from which to answer the chief questions of human existence: Scripture and the created universe, including human beings.

Thus the vision of human destiny unveiled in the New Testament book of Ephesians and insights from the contemporary "adult child recovery" movement form the two primary bases for our study. Generations of believers have discovered that the scriptural database provides indispensable perspective for making best sense of creation data, particularly when it comes to answering the prime questions. They have found that the quest for God and the realization of human destiny proceed best when the cosmos is viewed through the lenses of God's Word.

It also proves true in many cases that insight from the study of God's world provides new perspective within which to appreciate the force of God's Word. In the end, most insight emerges from a lively conversation between these resources. Chapters 2 and 3 outline the Scripture resources upon which we will draw. Chapters 4 and 5 sketch insights to be gained from the study of human beings and how they develop and relate to each other, particularly in families. Between the two we hope to launch a life-transforming conversation.

2

Holy Love
and Human Destiny

Scripture through New Eyes

Because of its striking clarity and its unusual relevance to the
main agendas of Christian discipleship and the process of
recovery from addiction and codependence, we will confine ourselves
to the Apostle Paul's letter to the Ephesians. Such a restricted
database would not do for an exhaustive inquiry. But even this
brief document will provide plenty of grist for our purposes. We
will take care not to draw conclusions which would be overturned
by such a larger study.

Getting Our Bearings in Paul's Letter to the Ephesians

Paul addresses himself to believers living in the capital of the first-
century Roman province of Asia Minor and its environs. He aims to
help these first-generation Christians chart a new life-course out of
the delusion and self-destruction of their culture (4:17–18; 5:6–14)
and on to a realization of their destiny of holy love (1:3–14; 4:11–16).

To appreciate the force of Paul's approach to matters pertinent
to the recovery-discipleship processes, we must take the work

seriously as a whole. We will do our best to keep this whole in mind, even though we have space to give attention only to those parts most directly related to our concerns. We begin with an overview of the letter's content and structure, i.e., what's in it and how it goes together. Hang on! We might picture the main units this way.

1:1-2	Greetings		
1:3–14	Intro: God's Purposes for Us		**Purpose and Potential of Love**
1:15–23	Prayer for Insight		
2:1–22	Their Story in Grace	*Biographic Reminders*	
3:1–13	Paul's Story		
3:14–19	Prayer for Roots in Love		
3:20–21	Doxology		
4:1–16	Call to Maturity in Love		**Christians' "Walk" in Love**
4:17–24	Break with Pagan Values		
4:25—5:2	Agendas for Living Holy Love	*Retrieval of Relationships in Love*	
5:3:14	Repudiation of the Darkness		
5:15—6:9	Life in the Spirit: Role-Specific Instruction		
6:10–20	The Battle		
6:21–24	Closing		

Here is how the units go together. Using a grand introductory blessing (1:3–14), Paul sketches the destiny of holy love that God wills for His people and the historic and present acts of God's grace on which that destiny rests. The realization of this destiny in his readers here and now becomes the recurring concern of Paul's letter. Two prayers reveal the means by which this destiny will be realized in his readers: insight (1:15–23) and roots (3:14–19). A reframing of their own story and his in terms of God's grace (2:1–3:13) and a concluding doxology (3:20–21) support the claims implicit in the opening blessing and the prayers. These pieces would have reminded Paul's readers of shared worship experiences. They provide theological foundation for practical teaching to follow.

Upon this foundation (1:3–3:21) the writer builds his instruction (4:1–6:20), reasoning from cause to effect ("therefore," 4:1). That is, "Since these realities of human destiny and spiritual resource I have written about are yours, I point you to life commensurate with them." General exhortation to unity (4:1–6) and maturity in love (4:7–16) opens this section. Over against this call to "grow up" (4:15), a contrasting general warning follows to break with the cultural norms of their old way so as to get on with the new life (4:17–24).

Then, reasoning from cause to effect again ("So then," 4:25), and moving beyond the general exhortations of 4:1–24, Paul issues his first specific instruction of the letter (4:17–5:2). In doing so he brings the force of his entire presentation to this point to bear on his readers' situation in these specific exhortations. These are strategic lines. It is almost as though[1] the apostle says (and here I beg indulgence for a "Pauline," i.e., paragraph-length, sentence), "If you want to realize the destiny God wills for you (1:3–14), if you want to experience the fruit of insight God gives (1:15–23) and enter the journey of grasping love's implications for which I have prayed (3:14–19), if you wish to build on the miracle of your own transformation and the point of my own ministry (2:1–3:13), if you want to achieve the unity and growth in love I have set before you (4:1–16), and if you want to break with the values of your pagan background, being done with the old way and getting on with the new, being 'renewed in . . . your minds,' and being 'created according to the likeness of God in true righteousness and holiness'—if all this, I say, is what you want, then tackle these issues: 1) 'Putting away falsehood, let all of us speak the truth,' 2) 'Be angry but do not sin' [in the process]," (AOT) and so on.

Following these core agendas of holy love, the apostle turns again to delineating the ways of "darkness" they must reject if these habits of the new way are to be realized (5:3–14). This exposé of the darkness intends to guide a counterculture lifestyle. Having set living "as children of light" (5:8) over against the pagan darkness, Paul moves to elaborate positively this life in "the light" (5:15–6:9). The unit centers around his exhortation to "be filled with the Spirit" (5:18), which controls a series of lines expounding that life in the Spirit—"speaking to one another . . . singing and making music . . . giving thanks . . . submitting yourselves to one another in reverence for Christ" (5:19–21 AOT). Then, picking up the last item in this expansion on life in the Spirit, he details the concept of mutual submission in role-specific instruction (5:22–6:9). The body of the letter closes with a summons to take up arms through prayer in order to stand victorious in the spiritual warfare in which believers find themselves (6:10–20).

Good News: God for Us and Destiny Worth Fulfilling (Ephesians 1:3–14)

"Why is God doing this to me?" "Where is God now?" Hurting persons often discover long buried distrust and anger toward God. Some in recovery find it difficult even to lift their heads in prayer, to look God "straight in the eye." Abuse or neglect at the hands of a caregiver or other persons who took on god roles for them— became powers beyond which they had no appeal—have badly tarnished the words "God" and "Father." The very first lines of this letter address these deep wounds. There we discover God passionately *for us*, decisively *on our side* from day one and for all time!

God Chose Us That We Might Be . . .

Paul's doxology shows two over-arching concerns regarding human destiny: 1) the transformation of human beings in holy love; and 2) the resulting realization of praise to God and His amazing grace. Verse 4 stands out: "According as God chose us in Christ before the foundation of the world to be holy and blameless before him in love" (AOT).

The short of it is this: the praise centers on God's choosing of "us" in Christ, and on the purpose of that pre-cosmic choosing, that we would be "holy and blameless before God in love." The rest of the doxology elaborates God's saving acts, which flow in one way or another from this purposeful choice, and its results for those who have believed the good news. The remainder of the letter addresses in one way or another the realization of this purpose.

In Love

We read, "Chose us so that we would be holy and blameless before him in love." Book context, Pauline theology, and literary style in this letter show that the apostle intends "in love" as a statement of the sphere in which God purposes His people to be holy and blameless before Him. (We should attach it to the preceding material, not the following lines as some recent versions do.)

All of this is marvelously good news, especially to persons accustomed to seeing God's "choice" of them as more of a curse than a blessing, something like the Army's "choosing" you. Persons accustomed to relegating "holy" and "holiness" to odd religious behavior, to marathon commitments, to church work, and the like will find this refreshing. The sort of "holy and blameless" life God desires will appear in authentically and truly loving human relationships.

"Holy" describes what belongs to God, what is totally and without reservation given to God. Like the word "holy," the word "blameless" has its background in the Old Testament. It describes the physically "flawless" sacrifice God desired from His people. Together here they describe the character appropriate to persons who "belong" to God. But get this: the apostle places these two terms, "holy" and "blameless," under the umbrella concept of love.

Paul's letter will examine the holy through the lens of love and will understand love as the primary and most meaningful expression of Christian holiness. To be holy and blameless before God is to be loving. To be loving is to be holy and blameless before God. Ephesians knows no authentic love that is not holy nor holy life that is not loving. Because of this connection we will talk most often of "holy love."

Human Destiny

This vision of persons as truly loving and thereby holy and blameless before God is God's dream for us. To this love God aspires for us; that we might come to this end He has chosen for us. What a marvelous discovery! This destiny matches the Creator's dream for His people implied in the Bible's creation story (Gen. 2:4–25). Like an artisan, God shaped His "man creature" and breathed life into him. At the climax of the story the first man and woman, fresh from the Creator's hands, stand "naked and not ashamed" (Gen. 2:25 AOT). Open, unafraid, vulnerable, nothing to hide, confident, caring—what a destiny! What a dream! God plans to recapture that dream for us!

The Problem: More Than Maladjustment

So what's the problem? Why the need to recapture that dream? Paul knows "the rest of the story" in Genesis! The dream dissolves in human distrust of God. The pair celebrated as "naked and not ashamed" (Gen. 2:25) become "nude and afraid," alienated from their Maker and masked from each other (Gen. 3:1–10). Paul knows that family dysfunction and personal maladjustment constitute symptoms of a much deeper problem in the human family—distrust of God and alienation from Him.[2]

So Paul's opening vision assumes persons not "holy," i.e., persons who do not live with a sense of belonging to God, who need to be brought home. He implies persons not "blameless before God in love," i.e., persons condemned before God and who need forgiveness and reconciliation. Thus he dramatizes God's historic initiative on our behalf in a series of pictures that emphasize our root problem of alienation from the One who made us. "Adoption" (Eph. 1:5), "redemption" (1:7), "forgiveness" (1:7), "made known to us" (1:9), gave us an "inheritance" (1:11)—all speak facets of the good news. And they all imply a prevailing "bad news." We are orphaned from God and need a family (adoption). We are hopelessly in bondage and need someone to release us (redemption). We are morally in debt (forgiveness). We are spiritually disinherited and in the dark (inheritance and revelation). We have deep problems that only God's grace in the end can meet.

But the trite and trifling content of much of the church's call to "make a decision for Christ" or "get saved" or "be born again" or "join the church" or "make a profession of faith" or "take the hand of fellowship" or "get confirmed"—these show the church has largely forgotten the meaning of "saved" and "salvation." Concentrating primarily on the good news of being set right with God through faith alone, the church has forgotten the scope of

God's plan. It has seriously narrowed the range of the rescue project God plainly intends in the good news. "Saved" has come to mean largely "not going to hell," "having eternal life" in terms of life after death, getting "set up" with God.

According to Paul in Ephesians, salvation has primarily (though not exclusively) to do with life here and now, with the whole project of human moral and spiritual transformation. God has in mind nothing short of the full renovation of human character. God proposes to radically transform His people from persons locked in behavior at odds with Him and governed by unworthy motives and goals (as in 2:1–3) to persons "holy and blameless before him in love." To this project Paul devotes the bulk of his letter.

Praise

In the realization of this destiny of holy love the other goal of the entire project finds at least partial fulfillment, namely that our lives would constitute a grand symphony of praise to God's grace (1:6, 12, 14). This claim constitutes the second major concern of the blessing, as the repetition and placement in the final line of the doxology show.

Judging by the lengths to which Paul goes to support his readers in continuing their journey and picking up the pace of their trek, the scope of the transformation project must have seemed daunting to them, as it does at times to us. Anticipating this he already reminds them in this opening doxology that they have been "marked with the seal of the promised Holy Spirit" (1:13). This seal, like an impression of the king's signet ring in the wax on state documents, shows ownership and identity. The Holy Spirit, given to all believers (3:20) and active in all who name Jesus as Lord (1 Cor. 12:1–3, 12–13), actually accomplishes in these people sufficient moral and spiritual transformation to demonstrate that these persons really do belong to God! They are holy (Eph. 1:4).

Moreover, this authenticating presence of God's Spirit Himself indicates that our faith in the whole gospel is valid. The Spirit Himself constitutes a "pledge" (1:14). The reality of the Spirit's character-transforming presence is a "down payment," guaranteeing that the gospel, with its far-reaching claims to the total, cosmic repercussions of the life, death, and resurrection of

Jesus Messiah, is not just a bag of beans. We have rather an authentic promise of the Living God!

Roots for the Journey (Ephesians 3:14–19, 20–21)

Paul understood what he called being "rooted and founded in love" (3:17 AOT) as the base from which the discipleship-recovery journey could proceed. The connection seems clear between this rooting in love and the love reorientation outlined in 4:25–5:2. This rooting provides the "strength," as Paul put it, to comprehend by experience the implications of God's love in Christ (3:18–19). These implications include exactly such things as the aspects of the discipleship-recovery journey charted in 4:25–5:2 (from delusion to disclosure, from destructive anger to dynamic motivation, from parasite to partner, from toxic talk to constructive speech, from rage to reconciliation, from abandoned waif to well-loved child). The "rooting" in love of which Paul speaks does not itself constitute the journey. But the rooting/founding does provide the commitment, the openness to the way of love that makes extensive progress in the journey possible.

This crucial planting of roots surfaces in the second of Paul's prayers in Ephesians (3:14–19). It contains three parallel petitions, the first two completed by parallel "to be/do" statements and interrupted by the strangely placed—and thus difficult to connect—but critical claim about being "rooted and founded." We can represent it like this:

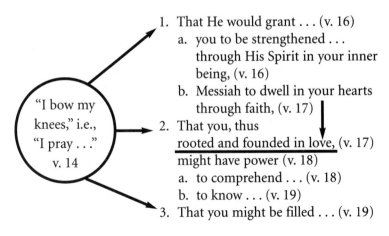

"I bow my knees," i.e., "I pray . . ." v. 14

1. That He would grant . . . (v. 16)
   a. you to be strengthened . . . through His Spirit in your inner being, (v. 16)
   b. Messiah to dwell in your hearts through faith, (v. 17)
2. That you, thus rooted and founded in love, (v. 17) might have power (v. 18)
   a. to comprehend . . . (v. 18)
   b. to know . . . (v. 19)
3. That you might be filled . . . (v. 19)

New *Roots for the Journey*

In light of this letter's purpose of leading these people to actualize the destiny of holy love for which they have been chosen and redeemed (1:4), one would expect their "rooting and founding in love" to have to do with that purpose. One would thus expect that "rooting and founding in love" to be not an existing condition assumed by the prayer, but a result of the prayer, specifically the result of the strengthening by the Spirit and the dwelling of Messiah in their hearts. This is why I have translated, "That you, thus rooted and founded in love [as a result of God's strengthening of your inner being by His Spirit and the Messiah's dwelling in your hearts through faith], may have the power to comprehend . . ." (3:17–18).

Also, in order for the prayer not to be pointless, the petition about Messiah's "dwelling" in their hearts must be understood as some sort of an advance over their present appropriation of Messiah's presence. Since according to Paul, Messiah by the Spirit already dwells in all believers (cf. Rom. 8:9, 11; 1 Cor. 3:16; Gal. 2:20), what sense, then, does this prayer have? Because of this I wind up paraphrasing: "That Christ may take up His abode in your hearts in some new, life-dominating sense [that will make possible the realization of God's chosen destiny for you]." This prayer, should it be answered, would root and ground these believers in love and enable them to get on with the journey of comprehending the real implications of living in love.

This implies another connection between the petitions, that the ability to grasp fully the implications of the love of Christ and to know by experience that love (petitions 2 and 3) results from, flows out of the strengthening, dwelling, and grounding (petition 1). The final petition (v. 19), to be "filled unto all God's fullness," is surely climactic and may be a summary as well, encompassing all the previous petitions while also going beyond them.

Discipleship—A Journey in Love

Paragraph and book context indicate that "love" is the object of the four descriptors in v. 18. Comprehending "the breadth and length and height and depth [of the *love* of God through Christ]" charts the path for the journey of Christian spirituality, Christian growth in grace, Christian holiness. The very nature of holy love makes the exploring of its implications an unending venture. This journey is rephrased in the parallel infinitive, "to know the love of Christ that surpasses knowledge" (v. 19). It captures the paradox of Christian spirituality. Those for whom and in whom this prayer is answered will actually know by experience the love of Messiah. And yet features of this love will evade them to the very end, for it is infinite.

I say "know by *experience*," for the word "know" entails more than cognitive awareness. They will actually experience His love for them and His love expressed *through* them to others. While the journey is unending and the complexity and depth of human sin is not to be minimized, this prayer envisions actual, thorough moral transformation in these pilgrims.

In this process they will "be filled with all the fullness of God" (v. 19), a mind-boggling prospect. Elsewhere Paul uses this word "fullness" to refer to Messiah Himself (4:13) and to the expression of God Himself resident in Messiah (Col. 1:19; 2:9)! As these believers are transformed in answer to this prayer, God will express Himself through them in ways analogous to, if surely not to the same extent as, His revelation of Himself through Messiah.

Roots through Trusting Messiah

Paul links this "rooting/founding" to the new presence of Messiah "at home" in our hearts by the Spirit (3:17). And he claims this transpires "through faith." Other persons can "enter" our mind/heart in two ways: 1) with our permission, as we entrust ourselves to them; and 2) without our permission, as they overpower or manipulate us. Dysfunctional caregivers and abusers enter our mental and physical person against our will or without our permission. God, and all other loving ones, "enter" our person with our permission through the door we open by trust. Thus, Messiah comes to be "at home in our heart" in the same way other persons "take up abode" in us—as we entrust ourselves to them, open ourselves to them.

Here we must stay with our context and not leap to vague notions of faith. And we must remember "faith" means more than agreement with a creed. Faith here means profound "trust." Each of the strands of the discipleship-recovery journey exposes issues in which disciples are asked to trust to Messiah affairs they have grasped tightly in their own hands.

- Can disciples entrust Messiah with the delusion they have brought to the journey?
- Can they entrust to Messiah their distortions of self, God, others, as they learn to speak the truth?
- Can they entrust to Messiah the protection they have achieved through the walls they have built, while they learn new boundaries?
- Can they entrust to Messiah the pain and shame they are covering with alcohol, food, drugs, sex, relationships, trinkets, spending, religion, or other anesthetizers?
- Can disciples surrender the leverage they achieve through rage and withholding and instead trust Messiah to help them build relationships that free others to choose their own destinies?
- Can they trust Messiah to help them get what they really need in life if they surrender parasitic ways?
- Can they trust Messiah to come through on His claim that if they authentically lose their lives they will really find them in Him and will not get caught again in rescuing persons and martyr manipulations?

These questions show that the discipleship-recovery journey is at the core a journey of growing trust. They also indicate that the rooting and founding in love would be a decisive, life-orienting entrusting of ourselves to Messiah that would critically open us to the succeeding acts of trust inherent in the journey.

Perhaps this rooting and founding in love can be likened to the recommitment to the journey common in marriages between the fifth and tenth years. Married long enough to see what they have actually gotten themselves into, couples often find themselves at a critical juncture. They must decide whether to actually go on with the journey or opt out. Will they entrust themselves to each other at the depth necessary to sustain growing intimacy, or will they leave in some way—outright divorce or settling into an increasingly superficial or actually estranged relationship hardly worthy to be called marriage?

Just as the foundational considerations open with a blessing (1:3–14), so now they close with a doxology (3:20–21). Following on the heels of the prayer, it forms a particularly significant conclusion to it. Paul may well anticipate his readers' response to these breathtaking petitions—disbelief, amazement, perhaps even discouragement. So the doxology encourages by reminding them that, as this prayer is answered, it will be God's doing by His Spirit.

The readers' attention is turned from themselves and their own need of these transforming workings of God in them to God Himself, to His Spirit continually active in their destiny, to His glory. They are drawn to look beyond their important but very small lives to the glory of God across generations.

Questions for Reflection

1. What resources have I identified for my own journey to this point?

2. Have I ever used my imagination to connect myself personally with the great acts of salvation the Bible talks about, to see myself as chosen, or myself as adopted, or the like?

3. Have I raced into the journey without "sitting" to soak up my identity as a child, dearly loved by God?

4. Have I ever confronted the deep question of my fundamental trust in Messiah, placing my entire life and journey in His hands, to root and found me in His love and pave the way for a lifetime of learning what His love means?

5. Have I pretty well restricted "faith in God" and "being saved" to believing "the truth"—escaping hell and going to heaven—when God calls me to trust Him so fully His Messiah is at home in my life?

Holy Love and Real Life

Rubber-Meets-the-Road Religion

Discipleship and recovery both demand more than lofty visions. So Paul draws real-time conclusions from the theology and vision splashed on the canvas in the first three chapters of Ephesians. Now in the last three chapters, he moves from a vision of holy love to ground-breaking instruction as to how that vision could actually come to reality in the lives of these first-century urbanites.

Unfortunately his "rubber-meets-the-road" transition can seem conspicuously absent in many churches. Presbyterian pastor Frederick Buechner expressed the lament of many hurting people when he described his response to the AA-like groups he encountered during his daughter's plunge into anorexia.

> I do not believe that such groups as these which I found my way to . . . or Alcoholics Anonymous, which is the group they all grew out of, are perfect any more than anything human is perfect, but I believe that the church has an enormous amount to learn from them. I also believe that what goes on in them is far closer to what Christ meant His church to be, and what it originally was, than much of

what goes on in most churches I know. . . . They make you wonder if the best thing that could happen to many a church might not be to have its building burn down and to lose all its money. Then all that the people would have left would be God and each other. . . . The church often bears an uncomfortable resemblance to the dysfunctional family. There is the authoritarian presence of the minister—the professional who knows all of the answers and calls most of the shots—whom few ever challenge either because they don't dare or because they feel it would do no good. . . . There is the outward camaraderie and inward loneliness of the congregation. There are the unspoken rules and hidden agendas, the doubts and disagreements that for propriety's sake are kept more or less under cover.[1]

Perhaps it is more than chance, then, that Paul turns his attention first in this half of the book to the supporting fellowship that can nurture the discipleship-recovery journey.

Supporting Fellowship (Ephesians 4:1–16)

Paul says God gave gifts to make possible the growth and unity summarized in 4:1–6. But surprise! These gifts God gave us are *people.* God gave us leaders as people gifts (4:11). And He gave us the community itself (4:15–16), with the leaders carrying the responsibility to equip the community to do its people-building work (4:12). Thus, loving persons in community are our most critical resource for the discipleship-recovery journey. As a matter of fact, we cannot make the journey solo for two reasons: 1) most phases require others for their execution (like playing tennis, as opposed to practicing tennis, requires a partner); and 2) the journey requires support.[2]

The sense of community and commitment to openness, vulnerability, learning, and building one another called for by Paul has kept many AAers and members of recovery groups coming back. Nothing humanly prevents the church from discarding its pseudo-mutuality and crowded isolation except the various strands of "the lie" confronted in the discipleship-recovery journey outlined by Paul. Persons committed precisely to that journey have great potential for becoming the leaven to enliven the whole community. And, in the providence of God and His ability to bring strength out of weakness, even the impaired can function to foster the journey in some way, provided sufficiently healthy leadership and core membership provide a "safe place" for them to contribute.

Family of Choice

Disciples must make some fellowship of believers their "family of choice," to give and receive the "building up in love" indispensable to the discipleship-recovery journey. When they do, they might well ask questions like these:

- Are the freedoms to feel and to speak in place in this group? Or are certain topics and feelings off-limits by definition? What happens when persons do not agree with the leaders?

- Does this group "level," or does it engage in sick communication?

- Do people actually listen and see each other here, or are they preoccupied with their single agenda—abortion, pornography, feminism, missions, education, faith healing, or whatever?

- Do persons here know the difference between authentically knowing God and being a Baptist, a Methodist, or a member of some other religious group?

- Does talk of God bring this group to face and solve problems or avoid them? Is prayer a matter of Christian "magic" here?

- Is the good news mostly hype here, or is there substance and thought to the teaching about it?

- Do people feel here, or do they just think? Do people think here, or do they just feel?

- Do scriptural concepts like holiness, righteousness, sanctification, truth, purity, and love receive specific "real-life" exposition or simply doctrinal pontificating and repeated generalization?

- In appropriate settings, do people talk about things that matter to them or about the weather, sports, and religious trivia?
- Do people show genuine affection for one another and exhibit long-haul commitment to and interest in each other?

This community, with commitment spanning the years and reaching across age groups and socio-ethnic boundaries, poses the single most potent resource at our disposal.

The Renewed Mind (Ephesians 4:17–24; 5:3–6:9)

Rejecting the Prevailing Culture's Mind

Recovery and salvation entail a battle of opposing and mutually exclusive cultural values and the basic belief systems they express. The destiny of holy love and the belief system it involves stood at odds with the prevailing values of the Greco-Roman culture of Paul's readers. So he immediately proceeded from his call to maturity in love to the contrasting instruction to break with that pagan past.

Paul focuses now on the "mind" and "understanding" (4:18) expressed in that culture. "Darkened" and "ignorant" characterize the mind of persons immersed in this culture (4:18). They stand accountable for their darkness and ignorance, because it represents compounded delusion resulting from multifaceted choices. It names a complex refusal to see (cf. Rom. 1:18–25).

Persons familiar with the "think-feel-do" cycle will not be surprised when Paul connects this moral, spiritual, and intellectual confusion with "insensitivity" (v. 19). He has in mind destructive and ultimately dissatisfying behavior in which persons surrender or evade accountability and use others. These cultural expressions involve, but are by no means confined to, destructive sexual activity. This delusion his readers know from their own past (2:1–3; 5:8).

Directly at odds with this life stands the journey opened by the good news of God's purposes in Messiah Jesus. "That is not the way you learned Christ!" says Paul (4:20). The "truth . . . in Jesus" (v. 21) they had been taught involved a repudiation of that darkness with its ways and entrance into the "walk" with Messiah (4:22–24), a profound and pervasive human transformation. The transformation involves assumption of a brand new personal identity. Paul pictures this as the "putting away" (taking off) of old, worn-out clothing and the process of "clothing" oneself with new garb as an expression of new identity.

The Renewed Mind

This "new self" represents no awkward "assuming" of an identity essentially foreign to the "real you" of these people. No. Paul talks here of their *minds* being *renewed*—cleared, calmed, ordered, informed. Information and belief structures to support the journey toward their new destiny will replace the confusion and corruption of their old life.

In the last analysis their new self can best be called a "new creation" (4:24). The mighty Creator will bring about in them the destiny for which He created the first humans. (Remember the "naked and not ashamed" of Genesis 2:4–25?) Altered belief systems and lived values are involved. But the new creation is more than simple "beliefs." The dynamic of this transformation is the presence of the living God by the Spirit, as this treatise makes clear elsewhere (1:12–14, 19–23; 3:16, 20–21; 5:18). The "new humanity" and the new creation from one perspective stand as accomplished facts of God's grace (2:15; 4:24). Their actualization awaits the trust of these believers.

With the language of "learning" (4:20) Paul brings us back to the concept of discipleship, which in the New Testament is essentially a learning process. In the New Testament a "disciple" is a "learner." "Discipleship" is the process of learning what it means to be a follower of Jesus of Nazareth by intentional engagement in the following itself. And the process focuses primarily on discovering by teaching and experience: 1) who Jesus of Nazareth is; 2) who His followers must therefore be; and 3) the nature and content of God's good news as announced by Jesus and expounded by His earliest disciples.

Paul now speaks of this discipleship process in terms of transformed identities (4:22–24). His language presents the "putting away" of the old life as something to be completed. This means a decisive repudiation of the old life with sufficient clarity to launch the journey of "putting on" the new self, of being renewed in the mind. At the same time, the repudiation is of necessity an ongoing endeavor. It involves the negative side of the continuing individual choices involved in appropriating the new way and actualizing the destiny of holy love.

The instruction "to be renewed in the spirit of your minds, and to clothe yourselves with the new self" (4:23–24) has explicitly in mind a lifelong process. Linked to their early reception of teaching about Messiah as "learning," this "renewing" is also a profound learning process. They will be renewed and clothed with new identity as they learn by instruction and by experience. They learn by reflecting on what they have been and are being taught of Messiah. They learn also by choosing beliefs, attitudes, and behavior consistent with "truth as it is in Jesus" (4:21 AOT), choosings which are themselves the faith process. In this process they will discover what it actually means to "be holy and blameless before him in love" (1:4). They will learn what "the breadth and length and height and depth" of Christ's love actually involves (3:18–19), what "righteousness and true holiness" expressed in human life mean (4:24 AOT).

Habits of Holy Love: The Discipleship-Recovery Journey (Ephesians 4:25–5:2)

To this learning process the apostle now turns his primary attention by moving from general instruction to much more specific exhortation and by tying the two together: "So then . . ." (4:25). The general instructions to "lead a life worthy of the calling" (4:1), and to "grow up in every way into him who is the head" (4:15), to "put away your former way of life" and to "be renewed . . . and to clothe yourselves with the new self" (4:22–24)—these general instructions now find specific expression in the more particular directions just ahead. In these instructions we find specific agendas of human moral transformation around which the concepts of "righteousness and true holiness," as well as the larger concept of "holy love," take practical shape and are given specifically Christian content.

This move to specificity brings us back to our view of the book as a whole. Now the overview might look like the chart above.

To Paul's amazing instruction on these features of the journey we will invest the bulk of our energy from here on.

Following this catalog of key behavioral and attitudinal agendas, three more sets of instruction remain, as we saw in the macro view

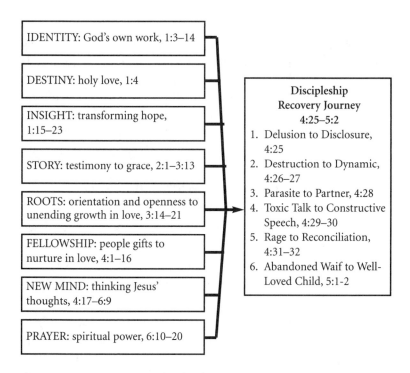

IDENTITY: God's own work, 1:3–14

DESTINY: holy love, 1:4

INSIGHT: transforming hope, 1:15–23

STORY: testimony to grace, 2:1–3:13

ROOTS: orientation and openness to unending growth in love, 3:14–21

FELLOWSHIP: people gifts to nurture in love, 4:1–16

NEW MIND: thinking Jesus' thoughts, 4:17–6:9

PRAYER: spiritual power, 6:10–20

Discipleship Recovery Journey 4:25–5:2

1. Delusion to Disclosure, 4:25
2. Destruction to Dynamic, 4:26–27
3. Parasite to Partner, 4:28
4. Toxic Talk to Constructive Speech, 4:29–30
5. Rage to Reconciliation, 4:31–32
6. Abandoned Waif to Well-Loved Child, 5:1-2

(5:3–14; 5:15–6:9; 6:10–20). The first unit contrasts with the positive teaching to live as "imitators of God . . . and walk in love" (5:1–2 AOT), and constitutes a radical exposé of the darkness of pagan life (5:3–14). Emphatic rejection of the vice-ridden, desire-dominated, degrading behavior of their old culture is supported by pointing out the utter incompatibility of these ways with "the kingdom of Christ and of God" (5:3–5). Strategic warnings against enemy propaganda, collusion, and behavioral compromise extend this teaching, urging life as "people of the light" in place of this darkness (5:6–14). The second unit begins as an elaboration of "walking as children of the light" of 5:8, with a series of exhortations to live astutely (5:15–16), discern God's will (5:17), and live in reality and health (5:18). This teaching leads the readers to capitalize on the providential time in which they find themselves. It urges them to avoid the traps of unthinking piety and addictive, dissipating ways by life full of God's Spirit.

The last of these concerns turns out to dominate the remainder of the unit. "Do not get drunk with wine, for that is debauchery; but be filled with the Spirit," Paul says (5:18). He then elaborates the exhortation to "live filled with the Spirit" with a set of clauses urging mutual encouragement and instruction (5:19), permeating gratitude (5:20), and mutual submission flowing from intentional devotion to Messiah (5:21). This last concept of "mutual submission" launches extended, role-specific instruction, showing how the Ephesians could "submit themselves to one another" (AOT) in husband-wife, parent-child, slave-master relationships (5:21–6:9).

Spiritual Strength through Prayer (Ephesians 6:10–20)

Disciples limited in their prayer repertoire to "Now I lay me down to sleep" or "Come, Lord Jesus, be our guest" will be surprised at this resource. But Paul concludes the letter with a three-pronged alarm regarding spiritual warfare, then leads the reader directly to prayer.

Forewarned Is Forearmed

First, the discipleship-recovery journey is spiritual warfare (6:10–12). It's spiritual and it's war! Everything in the book relates to that warfare. Just as God's purpose to integrate the entire, fractured cosmos in Messiah Jesus includes the healing of these believers' fractured lives (2:11–20; 4:25–5:2, etc.), so the cosmic spiritual warfare sounded in 6:10–12 includes the warfare in these believers' spiritual journey.

Second, we must have God's armor to stand our ground and be standing victorious at the end of the battle (6:11, 13–14). The defenses of distorted and deluded fallenness will not prevail in this battle. "Conventional weapons" will find themselves "out-gunned" in the battle. The war will go to those armed with truth, righteousness, the peace-bringing good news, trust, God's saving grace, and His Spirit (6:14–17). These weapons are implicit in the strands of the discipleship-recovery journey we have studied.

But third, this armament we take up only by prayer (6:18–20). Human effort alone to "get insight," to "be good," to "make peace," and so on will not do. The talk of prayer in verse 18, which looks in most English versions like a separate instruction, ties directly to the call in verse 14 to "stand." In other words, we take the armor and stand by prayer! This link could be translated best this way: "Stand therefore . . . by praying at every turn with all prayer and petition in the Spirit" (6:14, 18 AOT).

Prayer That Is Prayer

In order to see the power of this resource we must see the scope and power of prayer in Scripture. Paul mentions "petition," the "asking" sort of prayer most people think of first when they think of prayer. According to the Barna Research Group's work since the early 1980s, church people differ little in their prayer life from other Americans who claim no religious affiliation. Emergency prayer to solve physical or material problems concerns them most. Prayer as a resource for recovery expands this horizon vastly.

The book of Psalms showcases the sort of prayer Paul would have in mind. The majority of these psalms are prayers, but much more is here than petition. What characterizes these prayers most is: 1) their candor and direct approach to God and others, and 2) their breadth and variety, bringing all of life under the umbrella of prayer. Following the example of these prayers, we will include at least these agendas in our prayer life:

- Direct, plain-talk cries for rescue
- Honest reflection on life, and our life; processing in God's presence what we think of things
- Telling God exactly what we think of His role or apparent lack thereof in our life or the affairs of our culture
- Praying what we really think, not what sounds pretty or right
- Confession of sin without excuse or evasion
- Celebration of God the King and Creator and the amazing cosmos He has made and over which He rules
- Celebration and reflection on God's obvious hand in our life
- Rehearsal of our intense longing for God and His way
- Reflection on addictive, self-destructive ways

We have only begun. If we were to continue we would find prayer even includes unutterable groaning, the deep moans of the suffering soul in agony (Rom. 8:26–27). But this list points the way to learning to pray so that we view prayer as simply talking to God about everything in our lives in plain, everyday language.

Prayer Life/Life Prayer

"At every turn" or "at all times" Paul urges them to pray. On the run and at set times in their day they are to "care for ourselves" by turning home to God. They pray alone; they pray with others. But the armor gets put on by persons who actually live in prayer, turning to God repeatedly throughout the day. They do the majority of their praying with their eyes open! These disciples bring to God their feelings as they feel them, their questions as they have them, their anger as they experience it, their victories as they come. They pray not only for themselves but for others around them. They "think through" problems in prayer, make plans for the journey in prayer. "In everything, by prayer and supplication . . ." is no exaggeration for them (Phil. 4:6).

Prayer is no substitute for the journey or for the learning and choosing discussed in our considerations of 4:25–5:2. It provides the context for that learning and choosing. I recall times in the middle of my darkness when I could not pray for myself—for God seemed too distant. At those times, believe it or not, I prayed the prayers of others, like Jesus or Paul from the Bible, or like John Wesley, eighteenth-century reformer and founder of Methodism. As I prayed Jesus' prayer, I voiced surrender, confession, confidence I did not really have, but knew I desperately wanted. As I read Wesley's prayers morning and evening, he voiced what I, in my deep confusion, could not put into words. I even wound up praying some days for "the Queen"! But God understood. These saints carried me through until I could pray for myself again, and even then enabled me for the journey.

So we have resources: an identity to sustain our inquiry into our past and present; insight to bring hope; roots to provide orientation for the journey in love; fellowship to instruct and support; and prayer to clothe ourselves with the armor of God.

Questions for Reflection

1. Have I expected God to give me insight directly—slam-bang—without opening myself to the many information resources He has provided to open my eyes?

2. Have I reflected on the heavy-duty things I've experienced—divorce, kids' troubles in school or with the police, fights at home and work—to let God open my eyes?

3. Does my church act more like a dysfunctional family than a fellowship of healthy, caring, honest people? If so, what should I do?

4. Have I resisted "getting involved" in my church and thereby cut myself off from perhaps the chief resource for the journey?

5. Am I a part of any group of believers where freedom prevails and prayer like real "Bible prayer" is encouraged?

The Human Connection and Its Problem

Insight from the Human Connection

"**D**ad, I think this book might interest you," our oldest daughter Gina said. What an understatement! It was the fall of 1989; our family had just spun out of control into its "reality crash." She had been reading *Bradshaw On: The Family*[1] on loan from a classmate at Asbury College. Bradshaw's book had helped her make sense out of our family. She saw me groping for handles and thought Bradshaw had some. The Family Renewal Center (FRC), to which our family turned, guided us with concepts including those Bradshaw wrote about. In the space of about two weeks, the lights went on in my darkness. The information I was receiving in treatment at FRC and from Bradshaw at home at night as I poured over his work converged to provide a breakthrough glimpse of myself and our situation.

It was as if our reality crash had thrown me high in the air, while at the same time Bradshaw and FRC shot up reconnaissance flares, lighting up the whole terrain. The flash was bright enough to reach back years and enable me to see the relationship between items that to this point had either lain hidden or had sat as isolated dots on my map. Now I could see these isolated dots had paths

connecting them, some well worn to deep ruts! I had never perceived those ties before. Unfortunately it was not a lovely scene. But
there was hope. The "creation resource" had opened the door to
that hope, using the lever of my deep pain and fear. Bradshaw had
helped me see, as I had not been able to grasp before, the complexity and importance of the interconnections human beings sustain with one another, "the human connection." Specifically he
pulled back the curtain on my human connection.

This information resource also transformed my reading of
Scripture and theology at several points. The seriousness and
complexity of the issues of human life and existence with which
biblical writers deal were brought forcefully home to me. Real-life
content for concepts such as sin, salvation, grace, and sanctification moved these from theological abstractions to life and death
issues of survival for me. They had been so all along, but it was the
creation database and my own participation in it that made these
concepts so for me.

Alcoholics as Normal?

This also became clear: the problems separating truly troubled
and dysfunctional families from "normal" families—even normal
Christian families—are problems different in degree but not in
kind. This is what makes the bringing together more closely of
"recovery" and discipleship so important. As we pursue the creation resource we will talk much of the families of alcoholics and
other addicts and families housing schizophrenic or truly disturbed persons. Such talk may lead some readers to conclude prematurely that this book is really about someone else's problems,
since their family contains no alcoholics, drug addicts, schizo-
phrenics, or the like.

To conclude that all this talk of "recovery" is only for addicts
would be a great mistake for two reasons. First, in their tragedy the
"worst case" families have chiseled in bold relief the problems
which surface in less obvious fashion in "normal" families.
Second, these truly troubled families expose for all of us the deeply
serious, truly lethal nature of our "normal" problems. They
remind us that all sin is destructive, that all wandering from the

Creator's loving purposes is lethal. They encourage us to take much more seriously the apostle's instructions for life in Christ.

Creation Database

"Creation database" refers to the information we can derive from studying the universe God has made, including human beings. The sages of Israel studied all nature, including insects, reptiles, animals, human beings, and did so convinced that wisdom was to be gained by such study carried on in reverence for the Creator. The biblical book of Proverbs is one result.

Because we live in a fallen world, studying human societies as they are now constituted will not present us immediately with a vision of life as the Creator intended it. Beyond that all "data" must be interpreted, so wisdom counsels caution in drawing conclusions from the observation of human beings and their behaviors. Risks notwithstanding, this resource rewards careful study.

Psychiatrists, psychologists, counselors, sociologists, social workers, physicians, and anthropologists carry on this endeavor in our day, often, lamentably, without reverence for the Creator. For this reason and others, many are justifiably suspicious of the use of psychological "insights" by the church. They warn of the perversion of the gospel and the co-opting of the church by therapy and therapeutic approaches to ministry.[3] But the study of human beings still yields wisdom for believers when the gospel itself is clearly understood. The main claim that counselors of various sorts have to our ear is their monumental investment in careful "people watching" and studied reflection on what they have seen.

Gathering the Information

Over the last sixty years several streams of "people watching" have converged to provide unprecedented insight into human personal need and the power of God through the good news to meet that need. For one thing, in the late 1930s and particularly through the 1940s and 1950s psychiatrists in England and the United States were becoming increasingly convinced of the need to work with families as units.[4] Their frustration at being unable to help children when they worked with them isolated from their families led to this insight and to a wide range of research and reflection on the relationship of families to the problems of individuals presented for therapy.

About this same time the recovery of two "hopeless" alcoholics in profoundly spiritual experiences launched the movement that was to become Alcoholics Anonymous.[5] Bill Wilson and Bob Smith's transformation in 1934 and 1935 had come through surrender and continuing obedience to God in the context of confession, prayer, restitution, and testimony in the Oxford Groups in New York City and Akron, Ohio. It had been sustained by continual contact with the powerful fellowship of those groups supporting their sobriety. Aiming to focus more narrowly on sobriety than on the broader agendas of Christian discipleship and wanting to establish a pluralistic fellowship, AA was established in June, 1935.

Early on, AA discovered the need to help the families of alcoholics, even recovering ones.[6] Bill's wife, Lois, and Bob's wife, Anne, began to apply the AA principles to their own lives. They discovered not only the importance of their enlightened support to their husbands' continuing recovery but also their own need for spiritual transformation and growth alongside their husbands. The families of the "AAs," as members called themselves, began to meet in tandem with the regular group meetings. They addressed matters later explored as aspects of "codependence." In 1951, groups (which had sprung up spontaneously all over the country out of the desperate needs of the relatives of the alcoholics in AA) were organized as Al-Anon Family Groups. These groups have become as numerous and widespread as AA itself, supporting hundreds of thousands of families of alcoholics in their own recovery.

A further development occurred as drug abuse became widespread in the United States. Many persons and agencies working with alcoholics, drug abusers, and their families found the Twelve Step program of AA applicable to drug abuse, and the modes of family support developed in Al-Anon and of treatment developed in family therapy helpful to the families involved. By the 1970s and especially by the mid-1980s these insights had been appropriated for the "treatment" of persons with a wide array of compulsive behaviors. The scope of "addiction" was broadened beyond alcohol and drugs to include addiction to sex, gambling, religion, rage, eating, love and other behaviors, substances, and relationships. Millions of persons have found help in the "recovery" offered by the many treatment and rehabilitation centers and by the countless "self-help" groups that use these insights.

The net result of these developments, which have many complex interrelationships with one another,[7] is the accumulation of considerable insight into the "human connection." Classical literature, including the Bible, abounds with evidence of the ancients' insight into the human personality and the family. Even so, our generation has acquired a veritable database not really available before. Millions of hours of "people watching" and attentive listening have paid off with a vastly increased understanding of: 1) the sorts of problems that frequently underlie alcoholism, drug abuse, and other compulsive behaviors; 2) the nature and problems of families commonly associated with persons troubled by these addictions and compulsions; 3) the nature of the family itself and its workings; and 4) the meaning of recovery and the path to it.

My lack of professional expertise will not support a technically precise or an extensive presentation of these understandings. But it may prove useful to outline those insights that proved most helpful to our family and to those students and advisees at the seminary, as well as friends in my "Unfinished Business" Sunday school class, with whom I have had opportunity to share them. In this chapter we focus on insights illuminating the core problem we face. Our next chapter will turn to answers, real and unreal, to this problem.

Insight 1: Families Are Systems with Roles and Rules

Family Systems

Perhaps the first and most comprehensive insight regarding the human connection to emerge from this century's "people watching" is this one. Families are living systems—developing, interactive, integrated, balance-seeking units, bigger than the sum of their parts. Families are not simply a collection of individuals, unaffected by other members in the family, capable of being isolated from the others and treated as though their problems or promise were singularly their own. Families live and die together. The attitudes, behavior, health, or lack of it of any member, particularly of its primary caregivers, affect the well-being of all other members. Even though family members are individually responsible for themselves and their own attitudes and behavior, there is no such thing in family life as attitudes or behavior that are strictly private or "nobody else's business."

Thus the family resembles the human body (cf. 1 Cor. 12:15–27). Its different organs and parts live together. They nourish and are nourished by one another and otherwise affect one another. They react to conditions inside and outside the body so as to maintain stability and health in the body.[8] Again, the family resembles a finely constructed, complex mobile hung from the ceiling by a string, its various parts delicately balanced. Touching any one of the parts sets the whole mobile in motion until, by and by, it returns to its equilibrium. Hold one part down or to the side, and the mobile will come to rest in a different configuration.

Roles

Early on careful "people watchers" identified roles assumed by persons in all families, including troubled ones.[9] These "roles" described customary ways of thinking and acting by which the person participated in the family and contributed to its stress and/or sought its equilibrium. Put in most general terms, the parents' natural role is to model: "how to be a man or woman; mothering and fathering; how to be a person; how to express feelings and desires. The role of children is to be curious and learn."[10] Thus a parent's roles include being a Teacher, Leader, Provider, Nurturer. A child's roles include being a Learner, a Grower.[11]

But in dysfunctional families children's roles become essentially defensive strategies for protection against the family itself.[12] Elaborating these "defensive roles" Sandra Wilson names the following: *The Responsible One/Family Hero* (who "believes he or she is okay only when doing something for someone or being 'good'"); *The Scapegoat* (who takes focus off parental pathology and family by running away, failing, stealing, drinking, using drugs, or otherwise acting out the family's anger and anxiety); *The Adjuster/Lost Child* (who gets no attention except through accidents or chronic illness, doesn't fit in, has difficulty making friends, seems socially immature, and open to control by others); *The Placater/Mascot* (who gets attention by being cute, provides comic relief for family, is often protected from family secrets, and is never taken seriously).[13] Donald Joy pictures some of these roles as they appear in adolescence as the *Fonzie, Peter Pan,* and *Aldonza* syndromes.[14] The "defensive" nature of these roles is easily understood when one realizes that in alcoholic and otherwise dysfunctional families roles like *Offender, Rebel, Tyrant, Addict, Smotherer, Punisher,* and *Blamer* describe parental roles.[15] The roles are not only defensive but are also forged by the family's needs.

Rules

Families also have rules—spoken and unspoken—that guide the family's life and, along with the roles, structure and govern its interaction.[16] In other words, who cleans and maintains the house, keeps its medical and financial records, and why? Who drives, and who sits where in the car? Who pays what bills and why? Who prepares meals and when? How are vacations planned and funded? How are children disciplined and for what? Who prays at meals and why? Who goes where at Christmas or other holidays? Who talks how to whom? Who enters whose room or space or body and under what conditions?

With some thought persons can generally state a number of their family's rules, especially those actually spoken and acknowledged by the family. As it happens, a whole host of *un*spoken, often actually *un*known rules carry even more powerful force in the family and govern its actions and attitudes in countless ways. All these questions and countless others are answered by the rules. Learning what the rules of one's family are and what those of one's family of origin were—making the implicit, unwritten, unspoken rules explicit—will present a significant picture of the family.

In healthy families the roles and rules develop and adapt to changing situations while maintaining continuity. Troubled families, in contrast, exhibit rigidity and fragility. Roles become traps—fixed ways of responding to conflict or pain or threat or change—that lock individuals into certain functions for their own survival and the preservation of the family's stability. Rules become ruts, often hidden under the rug where they continually trip and snare the unwary.[17] Communication patterns in the family are the most important barometers of the health of the family system, its roles and rules.[18]

The Critical Marriage Core

The critical component in family systems is the marriage bond. A healthy marriage relationship, structured by "people-making"[19] roles and rules versus "people-breaking" relationships, forms a core around which healthy relationships can be developed with and between succeeding children which may appear. Murray Bowen observed that in all the families he studied there was a "striking emotional distance between the parents" which he called "emotional divorce."[20] This emotional "divorce" and the individual needs which produced it block the development of consistently healthy relationships. And they generate skewed and damaging relationships among all members of the family.

So families are systems with roles and rules which either nurture or destroy persons. Already implied in the claims about the critical role of the marriage partnership and its impact on children born to it is the insight that family systems involve multiple generations and the relationships between them.

Insight 2: Problems Are Intergenerational

Transmitting Fallenness

Further family research has confirmed the fact that personality traits, healthy and unhealthy, are transmitted through the family system one generation to another over multiple generations.[21] Thus ways of communicating, of defining roles, and of formulating the spoken and unspoken rules of the family are passed on to succeeding generations for good or ill.

This intergenerational linkage in family personal and spiritual health appears clearly when it is graphically presented in a genogram.[22] A genogram is a sort of family tree, keyed to indicate the presence of various traits and symptoms of mental and spiritual dysfunction. One can use different kinds of lines (straight, wavy, dotted, etc.) to show different sorts of relationships between people (normal, disturbed, broken), and symbols or abbreviations to flag individuals for various addictions (alcohol, drugs, sex, eating, work, religion) and other compulsive behaviors or chronic illness.

Just such a chart brought home to me how the "inheritance" of alcohol and drug abuse, sexual dysfunction, and broken relationships that laces my extended family of origin surfaces now and again in my own family and that of my brother and sister! A genogram also reveals the traces of grace and salvation operating among these generations. Persons who manage to emerge from dysfunctional families with surprising balance and maturity stand out. The impact of life-changing, spiritual experiences on persons clearly can be seen.

Just how fallenness is transmitted from generation to generation remains in some ways a mystery. But these lines of transmission show the communication of human fallenness through human relationships to be one major means. Genetic factors may well be involved. But impaired parents clearly impair their offspring by the very ways they relate to them from the start.

Problems Marry Problems

Not only are family personality traits, good and ill, transmitted intergenerationally, but new families are created which guarantee the perpetuation of the larger family's problems, as though by a hidden but nearly irresistible force. As Bradshaw describes it, "Dysfunctional families are created by dysfunctional marriages. Dysfunctional marriages are created by dysfunctional individuals *who seek out and marry each other*" [emphasis added].[23] Of course no one in their right mind wants to replicate the tragedies of their childhood in their own families. Middleton-Moz explains it as a process much like that in which a person from another culture might choose a partner with familiar language, customs, and values. We choose persons who let us "be at home" emotionally and behaviorally.[24]

Simply put, the cycle of addiction and dysfunction looks something like this. It operates like a self-perpetuating contraption unless stopped by interventions of healing and grace.

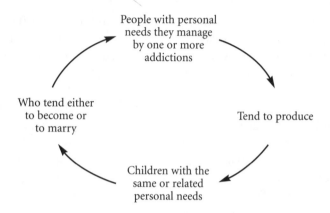

Insight 3: Core Shame Is the Problem

Core Shame

Long term "people watching" with alcoholics and drug abusers has revealed that significant numbers of these persons had a more fundamental problem than their alcohol and drug abuse. As a matter of fact, their alcohol or drug abuse proved primarily to be a symptom of the more fundamental problem, much like shortness of breath or kidney problems may be symptoms not necessarily of lung or kidney disease but of heart failure. This more fundamental problem was an inner deprivation perhaps best characterized as "core shame." "Core shame" refers to shame about one's very self—not appropriate shame about one's behavior or about specific traits.[25] "Core shame" names a "Not OK" identity owned in earliest childhood and, without intervention and help, carried through life.

Abandonment

What produces this fundamental problem of core shame? Emotional "abandonment."[26] Raised by parents or other primary caregivers who are addicted to alcohol, drugs, or to any thing/one else, or who are otherwise seriously impaired emotionally, many children find themselves abandoned emotionally and often physically by their caregivers.

The flow of emotional nurture in such families is effectively reversed. Instead of the children's needs being met by their parents, the parents' emotional needs are met by the children. From infancy, children in such homes learn to respond not primarily according to their own needs and wants, but by what pleases their parents. This involves much more than learning appropriate respect and obedience. They do what enables them to survive in their home. Such children in effect give themselves away before they have ever taken possession of themselves. The more dysfunctional and abusive or unpredictable their primary caregivers, the more completely these little ones lose themselves in the quest to accommodate their parents.

These children literally forfeit the opportunity to experience key developmental tasks necessary for progress to the next step of maturity! They in effect "skip" much of childhood and/or adolescence and wind up as adults without having completed the developmental tasks.[27]

Tragically, such children not only lose themselves but *blame* themselves for the inadequate parenting they experienced. This idealization of one's parents appears most starkly and ironically in the well-known cases of sexually and physically abused children. Such children often actually blame themselves for the reprehensible behavior of their caregivers while repressing the memory of their abuse as it actually occurred. The result? Self-loathing, loss of self-esteem, i.e., core shame.[28] These same transactions skew more "normal" troubled families as well.

Parental Good Intentions

Although, sad to say, deliberately destructive parents can be found, most parents set out to do the best they can with the tools they have. Realizing what I had done to my own children was one of the most painful awarenesses ever to dawn upon me. In many cases abandonment occurs in families *not because of but in spite of their best intentions.*[29] This strange reversal often complicates the process of "good families" coming to grips with what has actually happened to them. This irony poses a particular trap for "church families" like ours or "synagogue families," where the pathologies that exist have been given an acceptable face by the influence of the faith.

So in our family, the superficial "ethos" of the family—carried by good intentions, much talk and thought of love, and abundant signs of affection—masked the desperate neediness of the people trying their best to "live in love." The actual, relational structures of our family and the patterns of communication tracing them effectively sabotaged the good intentions and undermined the ethos to the point of collapse. In the end, what parents intended proves beside the point in assessing the initial impact of behavior on children. What actually transpired must be faced and dealt with if healing is to be found.

Thus abandonment, intended or otherwise, generates core shame. Core shame robs a child to one degree or another of the sense of well-being needed to mature and to develop healthy and satisfying relationships throughout life.

Insight 4: "Adult Children" Are the Carriers

Who Are "Adult Children"?

"Throughout their life"—that's the catch! As the information on intergenerational transmission of the family's problems implied, core shame is not simply a problem of little children. Age does not appear to alter significantly a little child's core perception of himself or herself.[30] Persons like Janet Woititz, working with the families of alcoholics and adults who grew up in alcoholic homes, came to realize that "although the suffering [carried by children of alcoholics] manifests itself behaviorally in different ways, children of alcoholics seem to have in common a low self-esteem" (the same concept as Bradshaw's "core shame" or Firestone's "self-hate").[31] They also came to realize that these adults from alcoholic homes exhibited sufficiently serious, common, and specific problems as to merit identification as a population deserving specific attention. Thus Woititz coined the identification of these persons as "adult children of alcoholic parents" (ACAP)[32] or "adult children of alcoholics" (ACOA).

Characteristics

From the generalizations that recurrently surfaced in the groups of adult children of alcoholics Woititz worked with, she profiled the following self-perceptions as worthy of careful attention. Adult children of alcoholics repeatedly described themselves as persons who:

- Guess at what normal behavior is
- Have difficulty following a project through from beginning to end
- Lie when it would be just as easy to tell the truth
- Judge themselves without mercy
- Have difficulty having fun
- Take themselves too seriously
- Have difficulty with intimate relationships
- Overreact to changes over which they have no control
- Constantly seek approval and affirmation
- Usually feel that they are different from other people
- Are super responsible or super irresponsible
- Are extremely loyal, even in the face of evidence that their loyalty is undeserved
- Are impulsive

These insights have been confirmed and expanded in other experience with this population and now surface in widely scattered publications.[33]

As did Woititz, Bradshaw concludes that the fact of these common characteristics "betrays an underlying structure of disorder." These persons "are not just reacting to the drinking of the alcoholic." They are "reacting to . . . the relational issues, the anger, the control issues, the emotional unavailability of the [parent] addict . . . a response to the trauma of the abandonment and ensuing shame that occurs in alcoholic families."[34]

Thus, "adult child" has come to carry a twofold connotation. First, it designates this specific population of persons, adults who grew up in alcoholic homes, i.e., children of alcoholics now become adults. Second, and moving beyond alcoholic families, it names adults with specific, common problems, the problems of adults living with unmet childhood needs and often driven by those needs. "Adult child" thus presents the picture of a needy child in an adult body. It pictures a "lost child" in search of himself or herself and the love, nurture, and instruction lost in childhood. Without intervention these children will tend either to become addicts or to marry addicts or otherwise bond to persons who enable them to carry on the "child's" quest for itself. "Adult children" carry the problem of core shame.

At this point some readers will, I suspect, have an experience akin to mine the night I began reading *Bradshaw On: The Family*. Looking at their own family as a system connected to a larger system, pondering abandonment and core shame, thinking of themselves or family members they know as "adult children" will open doors all over the place for them. Handles for problems that have eluded them for years might appear, at least in vague outline. Reasons as to why their difficulties have not yielded readily to simple confession of sin or general consecration of themselves may arise.

Happily, viable hope exists for all of us, no matter how tangled we have become. In our next chapter we turn to that hope, examining unsatisfactory, indeed destructive "answers" to the problems we have seen, and finally offering authentic hope in the discipleship-recovery journey.

Questions for Reflection

1. Because of the unfortunate work of some psychologists and sociologists, have I prematurely dismissed the revelation God wants to give through Creation as the domain of "secular humanists"?

2. Have I ever considered carefully the sorts of persons and problems found on my extended family tree? Have I ever pondered the significance of those persons for understanding my own situation?

3. Can I see couples throughout my extended family that seem to have been "tailor-made" for each other in very unfortunate ways?

4. Have I ever tried to identify the roles that persons in our immediate and extended family seemed to play?

5. Do I know the rules, spoken and unspoken, by which our family lived?

Hope for the
Human Connection

Answers, Real and Unreal

Reading Bradshaw I saw not only our family's problems but also glimmers of hope. Clearly we had dug ourselves a deep hole. But just as clearly there was a way out, though it would not be easy.

The last four insights from the "creation database" to which we now turn probe answers to the web of problems uncovered in the first four. The first "answers" turn out to be fool's gold, actually more of the problem. Exposing them is itself part of the answer. But finally we do get to truly good news. The good news of Jesus proposes a radical recovery journey that transforms persons mentally, physically, morally, and spiritually! The power of that grace presents more than a match for any human problem.

Insight 5: Addictions—Not Confined to Alcohol and Drugs—Are the Adult Child's "Answer"

Causes of Alcoholism

The cause of alcoholism remains a topic of debate and could well include genetic or biological, cultural, environmental, intrapersonal, and interpersonal factors.[1] Quite likely no single explanation accounts for all cases, and multiple causes may well be at work in individual instances.

Early on AA workers concluded that alcohol abuse was for many persons an attempt to "deny the underlying problem of life," as Kellerman put it.[2] Alcohol and drug abuse has now become widely recognized as an ill-fated attempt to deal with the insufferable pain of abandonment and the complications of self-destructive behavior arising from it. Such an explanation may not account for all cases of alcoholism. But the wide success of treatment based on this conclusion, and the vastly common "fit" of such an explanation with the biography of substance-addicted persons argues for the validity of the thesis as at least a partial explanation in many cases.

Extending the Idea of Addiction

Treatment counselors discovered that many alcoholics, already in AA and who had stopped drinking, wound up being "dry drunks," as William Sloan called it—persons who stopped drinking but continued "still drunk with . . . irrational thinking."[3] Addiction proved to be more than chemical dependence. It involved an entire addictive way of thinking and behaving. Eating, gambling, sexual activity, working, excitement, and other compulsive thought and behavior could serve the same goals as chemical dependency and could often be linked with alcohol or drugs, forming other layers of addiction. Even religious behavior could function this way. This has led to an understanding of compulsive/addictive behavior as "a pathological relationship with any mood-altering experience that has life-damaging consequences."[4] "Pathological relationship" means a destructive, controlling, delusional, and often incremental relationship with a substance, person, behavior, etc. *Destructive*—persons hooked on these are destroying themselves (and often others). *Controlling*—persons cannot "just say no" by sheer willpower. *Delusional*—persons delude themselves, deny, or rationalize the destructive consequences of their behavior. Often *incremental*—more and more of the substance, experience, etc., is required to produce the desired mood alteration. Increasing preoccupation with the addictive behavior often occurs.

"Workaholism" (addiction to work), for example, is not simply having a job that demands a lot of time or being committed to one's work. It is the use of work to counter or drown self-hate, to prove one's worth. It is work to evade the pain of intimacy, to avoid facing and dealing with problems, to establish control. One cannot just walk away from this relationship with work without "withdrawal." This approach to work destroys self and others.

Addiction to religion is not religious zeal or radical faith in action. Religious addiction involves at least the use of religious behavior or faith to avoid facing squarely past and present life problems. Addictive religion shifts from ourselves to God or religious authorities the responsibility God gives us for ordering our own lives and relating lovingly and authentically to ourselves and others.

Two critical findings emerge here:

- First, alcoholic families consistently produce in disproportionately high incidence not only alcoholics but the whole range of equally destructive, addictive/compulsive behaviors noted above. The abandonment and the profoundly broken relationships set the children of alcoholics up for these addictions.

- Second, this entire set of addictive/compulsive behaviors in families consistently produces the same intrapersonal and interpersonal effects as alcoholism. Children raised by workaholic parents, by religiously addicted parents, in sexually abusive homes, etc., suffer the same core shame (intrapersonal) and experience the same relational difficulties (interpersonal) as adult children of alcoholics. The addictions/compulsions function interchangeably.

The more general description, "dysfunctional," encompasses this whole set of pathologies. Life doesn't work this way! All the addictive, compulsive behaviors mask the adult child's core shame and represent totally inadequate "answers" to that problem and the others arising from it.

Insight 6: Codependence Is the Core of Addiction

Definition and Causes

People watchers first identified codependence by observing the irrational behavior of family members in alcoholic families.[5] These family members, who may even have brought the person in for treatment, would often actually sabotage the addict's attempts to maintain sobriety. Contrary to their alleged intent, they seemed unable to survive the loss of the alcoholic's addiction in the family. Other members, particularly spouses or adult children, continued to stay in intolerably abusive situations when, by leaving, they could have forced the alcoholic to face the consequences of his or her addiction.[6] These persons were actually "co-addicts," hooked on relationship with the addict itself.

Treatment personnel, counselors, and researchers soon realized that codependent relationships permeate all dysfunctional families. In *Released from Shame,* Sandra Wilson defines codependence as "a shame-based, painful pattern of dependence on others to provide a sense of personal safety, identity, and worth. Codependency binds us to relationships where we are being disrespected and controlled by people we, in turn, disrespect and attempt to control. It is 'other addiction'" [emphasis added].[7] Bradshaw coins the word "otheration" to describe this "loss of one's inner reality and an addiction to outer reality."[8]

Characteristics of Codependence

Like the addictions, codependent behaviors are survival skills learned by children to cope with abandonment. Unfortunately, the skills that allowed the child to survive prove to be shackles in the adolescent and adult world.

According to Pia Mellody, codependent persons exhibit five core symptoms. They have difficulty:

- Experiencing appropriate levels of self-esteem
- Setting functional boundaries
- Owning and expressing their own reality

- Taking care of their adult needs and wants
- Experiencing and expressing their reality moderately[9]

Thus, codependent persons:

- Say yes when they mean no
- Do something for someone although that person is capable of, and should be, doing it for himself or herself
- Meet people's needs without being asked and before they've agreed to do so
- Consistently do more than a fair share of work after their help is requested
- Consistently give more than they receive in a particular relationship
- Try to "fix" other people's feelings
- Do people's thinking for them
- Solve people's problems for them
- Protect people from the consequences of their own choices, and/or suffer people's consequences for them
- Do not ask for what they want, need, and desire[10]

Like the addictions, unfortunately many of these marks of codependence are encouraged by our culture. Some of them are mistaken for the marks of compassionate or helpful persons. And, as a matter of fact, before we are finished we shall have to distinguish these modes of living from the life of authentic love to which God calls us. Some may be necessary behaviors in specific, unusual circumstances. But these marks of codependence as consistent traits are not authentic love. Instead they spell trouble for individuals and families.

Codependency's link with the adult child's core shame is clear when we recall the source of that shame. Little ones in dysfunctional families are forced from earliest hours to give themselves away with the correlative self-rejection. They are led by their situation to become someone other than they really are or would be, were it not for the demands of surviving without adequate parental nurture and instruction. From day one adult children have been addicted to others, caught in "otheration." Thus codependence is the "root of any and all compulsive/addictive behavior."[11]

Insight 7: Resilience Is the Flip Side of Codependence, and That's Good News

Although the "survival skills" learned by children to cope with abandonment usually prove inadequate, even destructive when brought unreflectively into adult life, they are "skills" nevertheless! When adult children face squarely the damage done to them by their dysfunctional families, and when they learn the potentially crippling effects their hard learned "skills" can have, they can find themselves in possession of valuable assets to celebrate. Capacities of keen observation and penetrating understanding of human behavior, ability to take charge of their own situation and destiny, gifts in establishing and nurturing relationships, initiative in problem solving, imaginative creativity, humor, and moral sensitivity appear among these assets.

Steven J. Wolin and Sybil Wolin emphasize these findings in *The Resilient Self: How Survivors of Troubled Families Rise Above Adversity*.[12] The Wolins underscore two findings from their own work with troubled families and from the research they report on responses to adversity. First, children in troubled families are usually not simply passive victims of their situation. Even while their environment is exacting a heavy toll from them, these children customarily exhibit heroic initiative and creativity in carving out some corner of sanity in their chaotic worlds. They acquire coping skills from deliberate, sustained efforts to come to terms with the deficiencies in their families. This presents cause for celebration and provides a footing for reframing the past and recovering the present, often engendering something of a "Survivor's Pride" that bolsters recovery.

Second, Steven and Sybil Wolin emphasize that growing up in a dysfunctional family does not *necessarily* lead to decreased psychological functioning in adults. The Wolins find, on the contrary, that "children can cope with adversity and that, ironically, an increased sense of personal competence can result from success-fully meeting the challenges of a troubled family."[13] They reject the idea that adult children are best served by interpreting themselves as victims, doomed to repeat the pathologies of their parents.

The Wolins' optimism represents no psychological shell game where what once was called pain is now called opportu-nity. They do not just rename "liabilities" as "assets." Nor do they trivialize the toxic nature of dysfunctional families. Finding the resilience one's experience has fostered requires facing head-on the damage sustained in a troubled family.[14] Rather they insist that, having named the damage honestly, more is to be gained by "mining the gold" of one's painful expe-rience, as Donald Joy phrases it, than by endlessly rehearsing and reinforcing one's victimization.

The Wolins name seven resiliencies that survivors of troubled families often experience.

- *Insight.* They have learned to observe keenly, reject non-sense, and probe for underlying explanations.

- *Independence.* They have gained the ability to put emotional distance between themselves and their circumstances, to master their own inner situation.

- *Relationships.* They know how to connect with people.

- *Initiative.* Their goal-directed, problem-solving, self-start capacities set them up for effective work.

- *Creativity.* Their capacity to imagine and compose creates beauty and promise where others will see only problems.

- *Humor.* They "direct the urge to play into humor, mixing the absurd and the awful and *laughing* at the combina-tion,"[15] and produce gold for managing stress.

- *Morality.* Their suffered injustice has forged a precious sense of "holiness in an unholy world," as the Wolins put it.[16]

Adult children—survivors of troubled families— surmount the damage they have experienced by a process Steven and Sybil Wolin call "reframing." In reframing, the survivor "rewrites the script" of his or her family experience, reinterpreting their past so that the truth about the survivor's own journey becomes clear.

Insight 8: Recovery Is a Journey of Mental, Physical, Moral, and Spiritual Transformation— and It Is for Everyone!

Good news! As desperate as these problems may seem, hope abounds in the journey of personal transformation known as "recovery."

Journey

Recovery is a journey. Recovery names the process, by the power of God, of 1) gaining control of one's "out-of-control" life, 2) achieving sobriety from crazy-making ways, 3) facing the reality of unmet childhood needs which drive one's addictions and compulsions, 4) learning to meet those needs in ways appropriate to an adult, and 5) moving intentionally toward our destiny of holy love.

There Are No Shortcuts

There may be and often are dramatic points of insight and redirection. But recovery names a transformational journey that brings deeper and deeper healing and sobriety to the whole person. This may prove particularly daunting to addicts and adult children whose first instinct is to think in extremes of all or nothing. But impossible it is not! Both the biblical and creation resources endorse this hope.

Mental

Dysfunctional families live in delusion and far-reaching distortion of reality. Addiction and codependence are ways of thinking shot through with denial of the truth—first and foremost about oneself, but also about others, about life, about God. Recovery begins with insight—awareness at some level that life as it is being lived has gone terribly awry. It continues with learning the truth about oneself, about "normal," about relationships, about life itself, and about how God intended it to be lived to His praise and our great joy. So, of necessity recovery involves a radically different way of thinking, a mental transformation.

Physical

Addictive/compulsive behavior and codependence inevitably have physical ramifications, for the mind keeps no secrets from the body. Most if not all of the addictions involve chemical dependency of some sort. Alcohol and drug abuse obviously so, but many of the others involve addiction to adrenaline and other internally produced chemicals as well. Add to this the psychosomatic repercussions of self-hate, the secondary physical damage from some of the addictions, and the body language of core shame and codependency, and it is easy to see why recovery involves physical transformation.

Moral

Since the beginning, recovery in AA has involved moral reckoning. That addictive/compulsive and codependent behaviors are strictly personal matters of concern to no one else is an idea that cannot possibly be sustained. Persons are victimized and destroyed. Recovery involves facing not only the abuse, abandonment, and victimization one has suffered, but also coming to terms with one's own role as an offender, a spreader of the lie, an abuser, controller, manipulator, and user of others. Recovery involves therefore a process of moral redirection.

Spiritual

Addiction/compulsion and codependence are at heart names for alienation from God and His purposes. They often involve overt rejection of God. They always involve distortion of God and His person, and therefore alienation from God as He actually is and from life as He purposes it to be. Recovery is the process, then, of learning to live in the grace of God, learning to open one's heart, mind, body, and life to all the various vehicles of God's transforming power at work in the world.

Recovery as a journey of spiritual transformation does not primarily involve talk only about God or rediscovery of religion. Artificial categories of "sacred" and "secular," "spiritual" and "mundane" will not do in recovery, for all of our issues of mind, body, attitude, and behavior are "spiritual" matters. For this reason "spiritual transformation" is probably the most comprehensive and most adequate way of viewing the journey. From the core of our selves where we are buried in shame on out to the extremities of our lives, we learn to live in the stunning reality that we are God's lavishly loved children—this is the journey of spiritual transformation.

For Everyone!

The families of alcoholics and drug or gambling addicts are not the only ones to confront problems of the sort we have outlined. Millions of "normal" families struggle with difficulties much like those drawn more starkly in severely distressed homes. As a matter of fact, *God's Healing for Hurting Families* claims that Paul's outline of Christian life itself places "recovery agendas" squarely on the plate of every disciple of Jesus.

To the particulars of this journey we now turn, attending one by one to the apostle's astounding guidance in Ephesians 4:25–5:2.

Questions for Reflection

1. Have I missed the addictions evident in our family because I was thinking solely in terms of booze or drugs?

2. Have we actually wound up using our faith talk and God talk to *evade* our problems rather than to approach them squarely? Have we pushed off on God responsibility for choices that are clearly ours, not God's?

3. In our family, do we do other people's thinking for them, "fix" problems that are not ours, protect people from the consequences of their own choices?

4. Are there signs in my life that, were I to face my situation squarely, I might find a residue of resilience that God could use to His glory?

5. Am I prepared to launch the long-haul, discipleship-recovery journey—allowing God to enter layers and corners of my life that have to this point been blocked off from His grace?

Part Three

The Discipleship-
Recovery Journey

O ur culture carries a "great open wound," according to Jeffrey
Imbach. It is a crisis of intimacy.[1] Imbach claims "the recovery
of love" is the only healing for this gaping wound. This crisis of
intimacy also stands as a sad irony of our culture. Never have
generations seen more books, more tapes, more toys, more skin,
more talk about love and sex than the post-sixties' generations. Yet
these same generations have probably seen fewer truly meaningful
relationships, less truly significant sexual bonding, nurturing touch,
and authentic love than any previous generation. What a tragedy!

The Crisis of Love

As Imbach realized, this crisis of intimacy actually exposes a
crisis of love. Our biblical and creation resources converged to
confirm this claim. In our creation data, the crisis of fractured
families and persons enslaved to various addictions had at its
base a primal deprivation of love. This deprivation resulted in
fundamental alienation from oneself and others. And these
proved to be symptoms of alienation from God.

C. F. Midelfort, one of the pioneers in family therapy research, put it bluntly: "Learning, growing, maturing, and being well depend on giving and receiving love." He concluded from his wide experience with families that "the capacity to love" revealed "the degree of health or illness present in a person or a family."² Paul brings together two insights germane to Midelfort and Imbach's claims. First, he claims human destiny to be life "holy and blameless before [God] in love" (Eph. 1:4), and second, he presents the life journey as a quest to know by experience the full implications of the love of God's Messiah (3:18–19; cf. 4:14–16).

The Journey

Our resources converged at a second critical point: recovery on the one hand and the actualizing of our destiny of holy love on the other are both journeys. Both recovery and discipleship are processes of learning and growing in authentic love. Paul uses the journey language by calling the life of faith in Christ a "walk" (Eph. 2:10; 4:1, 17; 5:2, 8, 15 NASB) and by giving instruction that focuses on life processes.

Although Paul does not use the word in Ephesians or in any of his writings, I have introduced the term "discipleship" because of its importance to the concept of a life journey and because of its foundational place in Christian identity. This was Jesus' own term for His followers. In our records Jesus did not call people to be "Christians" or "believers" as such (although He surely called for faith). Rather He specifically called them to follow Him (e.g., Mark 8:34 ff.), and referred to His followers as disciples, construing Himself as their teacher (Matt. 10:24–25). As they did, they were known primarily as "disciples," which means "ones who learn," "learners." The disciple learned on the journey. Attention to the journey itself is thus called discipleship. These two points of convergence in our resources lead us to the claim that discipleship is in fact recovery, and that recovery at its best is Christian discipleship.

As we have seen, Paul's teaching on "the walk" comes forcefully to bear in 4:25–5:2 on the habits of holy love which comprise the discipleship-recovery journey (refer to diagram in chapter 3).

In the process of expounding key issues in the development of true holiness, the habits of holy love address the chief agendas of adult child recovery. The claim is not that the apostle has in mind all we will discuss in exposition of his teaching. We do propose, however, that the matters we pursue are in fact legitimate *implications* of the apostle's teaching and not essentially foreign to his actual intent.

We do not think the agendas are arranged in an order dictated by particular steps in a recovery program. These are not necessarily successive steps or ordered stages in the discipleship-recovery journey. Nevertheless, we are struck by the fact that the issues most pervasively relevant to recovery/discipleship bracket these teachings like bookends. Honesty issues (integrity, reality, delusion, denial) stand at one end (4:25); authentic love from an awareness of love at the other (5:1–2).

How separate but related journeys can comprise a single journey we can illustrate by our family's favorite trip from central Kentucky to the Great Smoky Mountains. In that trip we make one journey in elevation—from about 800 feet above sea level to over 6,643 feet above sea level at Clingman's Dome. We make another journey in topography—from the Blue Grass Plateau to the Great Smoky Mountains in the larger Appalachian chain. We make a journey from our home and its responsibilities to a campsite or cottage and a time of leisure. We make a zoological journey from possums and polecats to black bears and wild boars. We make a journey from Interstate 75 to four-wheel-drive-only roads. All these separate journeys comprise a single journey. The "journeys" described by the apostle in Ephesians 4:25–5:2 are in the same way strands of a single discipleship-recovery journey. To this "walk" we now turn.

From Delusion to Disclosure
(Ephesians 4:25)

Relatively Healthy Family . . . Reprise

"A relatively healthy family." That's what we had told Bettye Stull during our first interview at Family Renewal Center. So our son was using drugs, habitually truant, and failing his senior year in high school. So our oldest daughter, once bulimic, was still struggling with diet, battering herself with an "Olympic" regimen and stressed to the max to maintain her college 4.0. What if our youngest daughter was putting the pedal to the metal for life in the very fast lane as an eighth grader? And what if the few topics of any consequence about which Ede and I still talked were points of deep contention, with many significant issues in our marriage stalled in convoluted, protracted guerrilla warfare? Still . . . "a relatively healthy family" said it best, we thought. We actually believed it! It's called "delusion." Turns out it's no joke.

For the likes of us, Ephesians 4:25 was tailor-made.

The Teaching

Having put away falsehood as an entire way of life, live speaking the truth, because we are related to one another like parts of a single, living body (AOT).[1]

With these three clauses Paul throws every adult child and disciple of Jesus a "cognitive life raft,"[2] and launches the discipleship-recovery journey from the maze of delusion to an authentic life of disclosure. The three-step reasoning is simple but radical: 1) confront and be done with falsehood; 2) learn to speak the truth; 3) do so because of the realities of the human connection. So what's so hard about that!?

Repudiating the Darkness

The Problem of "Seeing" the Darkness

As did Paul's readers, we live in a culture permeated with futile thinking, darkened understanding, and lethal ignorance (Eph. 4:17–19). "Putting off the old way" (4:22 AOT) gets nowhere without confronting that darkness. As we have seen, the delusion of fallen culture involves much, much more than a point or two of erroneous doctrine or faulty morals (though these are significant). The futility of mind in which we are all caught to one degree or another—adult children with particular force—involves a complex, pervasive confusion. Utter delusion about who we are, about who God and others are, about what we have actually experienced, and about what reality actually is characterizes the codependent, addictive-compulsive life—i.e., much of "normal" North American life.

Repudiating the darkness poses a particularly difficult hurdle for adult children. Not only have they based their lives on a huge misconception and distortion of reality, but they have come now by second nature to devote considerable energies to perpetuating those distortions, to denying that *the* problem (core shame) and its related pathologies even exist. As our family said, scattered, bruised, and bleeding on the floor at FRC, "We're pretty healthy!" In spite of the pain one is facing, actually admitting one's plight can be incredibly scary.

Discipleship-recovery begins with awareness, with insight, with a shaft of light piercing the delusion and darkness. This awareness opens the way for the first of AA's Twelve Steps, "We admitted we were powerless . . . that our lives had become unmanageable;" and subsequent steps four and five, "Made a searching and fearless moral inventory of ourselves ... Admitted to God, to ourselves, and to another human being the exact nature of our wrongs." Without that awareness the journey does not even start.

Breakthrough Insight

How God shines that light into our darkness differs from person to person. Many have no idea they are wandering in darkness until they suffer bruises from bumping into dead ends. Substance abusers wake up one day and realize they don't recall living the previous week. They discover they have just killed someone while DUI, or realize that they have "quit" five times over the last year, or that their family and business are in shambles.

Others, like me and our family, whose addictions and codependence have been more socially acceptable or even perhaps responsible for their "success" in some ways, may find it even more difficult than drunks and druggies to see the darkness. They may realize, among many other signs of delusion, that they:

- Regularly *plan to fail*, by overcommitment and unrealistic expectations and planning. Nothing they regularly do relates to the things they claim are their most important goals.

- Are never satisfied with themselves or their work, never happy with what they do or produce. In the face of solid feedback they remain unpersuaded.

- Regularly show up late, no matter how much time there was for preparation and planning.

- Have no real friends among all their many acquaintances, and have no satisfying relationships with persons unless they are somehow "helping" them.

- Seem inevitably drawn to people who either abuse, desert, or demean them.

- See their children, one after another, struggling with eating disorders, involved in destructive relationships, being truant or disruptive in school, using drugs or alcohol.

- Find themselves trapped in despair and depression with no apparent circumstantial or physiological explanations at hand.

- Regularly feel "taken advantage of" in relationships and organizations but cannot seem to say no.

- Have just bounced four more checks.

- Live in chaos at home. Things just happen, if they get done at all.

- Have paid $10,000 for college tuition and are doing everything but take responsibility for their own education.

- Feel "empty," like there is a huge hole in their souls. Feel abandoned by God, in spite of a lifelong quest for Him.

They realize they are "out of control," though they never would have thought of it that way. They certainly have not changed, indeed do not appear to be able to change, in spite of repeated resolutions to the contrary. They realize they and their family have more than a few eccentricities or personality quirks. People are getting hurt—badly.

Or they may get breakthrough insight in some other way.[3] Through pain, through people, through reading, through grace—somehow the light must dawn sufficiently, enabling them to not only come to terms with the darkness but to want to be done with it as well.

Recovering Reality

"Live speaking the truth" was my translation to heighten the life process implied in Paul's expression, "speak the truth." In spite of the absolute importance of the breakthrough insights and radical commitment to the journey implied in "repudiating the lie," both this repudiation and learning to speak the truth are life processes. The discipleship-recovery journey from delusion to disclosure involves two sides of the same Kingdom coin: 1) learning the faces of falsehood so as to identify their presence in one's life, and 2) learning one's own reality in order to speak it.

Identify the Faces of Falsehood

We are apt to think only of "big time" lies here and miss the relevance of Paul's instruction to all disciples. More is at stake here than lying under oath in court or embezzling funds from the church (though experience proves there is often more "big time" lying going on than the disciple will want to admit or even be aware of at first). As we discovered in the creation database, the roles, rules, and communication patterns in families carry the fantasy of fallen culture. These roles, rules, and communication patterns are the faces of the falsehood that destroy human beings even in "good families." The more dysfunctional the families, the more shot through with delusion and falsehood these rules, roles, and communication patterns will be.

Identifying the faces of falsehood means learning enough about these roles, rules, and communication patterns that one can identify them in one's family of origin and, for adults, see them in the family and other relationships one now has constructed. This is the "cognitive life raft" Middleton-Moz referred to: information to help one make sense of where you have come from and where you are.

Begin with Yourself as a Child and Your Family of Origin

What roles peopled your family of origin? What was your role in your family?[4] Were you the Hero, the Responsible One who brought respectability and a sense of achievement to the family? Was there a Scapegoat in your family? Were you the Scapegoat— blamed for everything and acting in ways to incur blame and punishment? Were there addicts in your family—people controlled by alcohol, drugs, work, religion, gambling, sex, food, or other things or persons? Were you or are you apparently addicted to any of these? Was there a Placater, a Mascot, someone who provided comic relief, who could always be counted on to relieve tension with a joke or a clown routine? Were you the Clown? Was there a Myth-maker, a "good news girl or boy" who always put a good face on everything, made pain itself seem like a thing to celebrate? Were you that person? Was there a Blamer, who always made others responsible for his or her actions or made any issue a matter of blame and failed moral responsibility no matter what it was? Were you the Blame Dumper?

What about the rules in your family of origin? Particularly what covert or unwritten rules governed the family you grew up in? As Satir puts it, what "freedom to comment" did your family's rules allow? What could you say in your family about what you felt, saw, heard, smelled, touched, and tasted? Could you comment only on what should be, or could you comment on what actually was before you?[5]

Satir poses four questions regarding this "freedom to comment" that may help flush out your family of origin's unwritten rules:

1. What could you say about what you were seeing and hearing?

2. To whom could you say it?

3. How did you go about it if you disagreed or disapproved of someone or something?

4. How did you question when you didn't understand?[6]

What communication patterns prevailed in the family you grew up in? Could persons ask directly for what they wanted, or did they have to beat around the bush or depend on someone to read their minds? Did people in your family discuss ideas and issues or did they pontificate and lecture, without allowing discussion or question? Did persons shout and harangue about most everything, or unexpectedly, or under stress? Did your family converse mainly in sarcasm, sending double messages? Did your family talk about what God wanted or was doing when they really should have been talking about what they wanted or were doing? As we shall see more fully when we investigate the discipleship-recovery journey "From Toxic Talk to Constructive Speech" (Eph. 4:29–30), these and other modes of communication maintain and spread "the lie." They are faces of falsehood perpetuating delusion, whether your family saw themselves as liars or not. They may even be the cultural preferences for some regions of the country. No matter. You will not go far on the discipleship-recovery journey if you do not recognize these communication patterns for the poison they are.

Look at Your Extended Family's Heritage

What heritage did you really receive from your extended family? What models for family roles, rules, and communication flowed through your extended family? What addictive-compulsive, code-pendent ways of thinking and relating passed from generation to generation to your family?

Construct your own genogram and treat it as seriously as if you were looking for signs of heart disease, breast cancer, or other deadly genetic conditioning. Use an example like Bradshaw's[7] or just design your own. Work back at least to your grandparents. Include your aunts and uncles and their spouses, yourself and your siblings, and your spouses and children. Design ways to flag all the standard addictions (alcohol, drugs, sex, eating, work, religion, gambling, spending) and other chronic problems of health or personality. Flag divorces or relationships ended prematurely by death (suicide, accidental, natural). Show the sorts of relationships that exist(ed) between persons (normal, disturbed, broken, etc.). If you think you grew up in a "healthy family" or good "church family," but you discover an extended family littered with grandparents, aunts, and uncles riddled with more obvious addictions and pathologies, go back to your own family's rules, roles, and communication with a more careful eye. Your "healthy family" assessment may prove true, thank God. You may discover as we did, however, that while the gospel may have rendered your parents' pathologies more socially acceptable, it had not fundamentally changed the deep structure of the rules and roles perpetuated in their extended families.

Face the Unfaceable

Living in a fallen world means all children experience some abandonment and are the recipients of some core shame. (Remember, perfect parents never existed—not even in Eden. The fall preceded the children!) But if you identify many of the faces of falsehood in your heritage, you will no doubt have to face the reality of your own profound abandonment, the pervasive pain of your own core shame. Living in families where dysfunctional rules and roles prevailed means living in a family that abandoned its young and shamed them to the core, no matter what face that adult child now wears.

Your search may also lead you to recover awareness of physical or sexual abuse, and turn up whole new issues you will need to pursue by the grace of God. In some cases "speaking the truth" will mean confronting adults with this sexual, physical, or psychological abuse, bringing the family's "secrets" into the open. This, of course, will never be easy, but is probably necessary more often than persons are inclined to think, necessary to gain one's identity as an authentic adult beside a parent or relative who has dehumanized you. Such disclosures may be necessary to bring a halt to behavior still going on or to prevent possible abuse of still another generation. Disciples of Jesus seek to be redemptive in all truth telling. In situations such as these, it may prove difficult to predict the most redemptive course of action. Be patient. Don't rush, but don't back off from the journey.

Go Beyond Blame and Evasion

Some may interpret all this scrutiny of one's family of origin and family heritage as an attempt: 1) to blame one's parents or family for one's own inadequate choices, and thereby 2) to avoid responsibility for one's own life and troubles by playing the victim. Of course, such miscarriages of truth seeking do occur. But this quest for the truth is not about assigning blame or avoiding responsibility. The journey is about gaining insight, about piercing the darkness and delusion Paul warns against. We note again that these verses are not prayers asking God to do something, nor advice telling us how to get others to do something. They are exhortations addressed to us, calling us, the readers, to take responsibility for our own journey of discipleship-recovery.

Speak Your Own Reality

Speaking the truth boils down to speaking your own reality. It acknowledges the fact that whatever absolutes there are outside me and my system, I can speak of them only as I know them. My own reality includes my perception not only of myself but of all other things as well.

This poses more of a challenge than one might think, particularly for adult children. As Pia Mellody reminds us, codependent

persons carry among their core symptoms the difficulty of owning their own reality: their bodies, their thinking, their feelings,
their behavior.[8] They have become so accustomed to thinking
what other persons want them to think, so accustomed either not
to feeling at all or to feeling what other persons tell them they can
feel that they have little idea what they really do think or feel.

Adult children have constructed such elaborate defenses
against their own shame and pain that they literally do not see the
truth about their own bodies and their own behavior. They may be
obese and see themselves as attractively trim or think it makes no
difference what they weigh. They may be anorexic and literally
starved but see themselves as too fat. They do not have a clear picture of whether they look nice or not, are healthy or not, and so on.

How they are actually behaving totally eludes them. They
monopolize conversation and consider themselves sensitive listeners.
They rarely utter a word and think they talk too much. They spend
their entire lives in analytical head trips and think they are simply
rational persons. They stand too close to persons and think others are
"standoffish." They touch others inappropriately and never understand the consequences. Their speaking, eating, working, playing,
relaxing behaviors are very different from what they actually perceive
them to be, even if they are looking in a mirror. They have long ago
given themselves away and really do not know what they actually *do*
think, feel, and do. For these persons, Paul's simple exhortation to
"speak the truth" will entail major personal growth.

Renewing the Mind: Truth in Belief Systems

The discipleship-recovery journey presented in Ephesians
4:25–5:2 charts specifics of the transformation which Paul called
being "renewed in the spirit of your minds" (4:23). This emphasis
on the mind, together with Paul's rejection of futile, ignorant
thinking (4:17–18) and falsehood, and his endorsement of truth-
speaking connect Christian discipleship firmly to clear, rational
thinking. Learning and living "truth as it is in Jesus" (4:21 AOT)
goes 180 degrees in the opposite direction from the convoluted,
deluded, obsessive, inverted, distorted thinking of addiction,
compulsion, and codependence. Abandonment with its ensuing

core shame and life fantasy take a horrendous toll on thinking capacities. Obsessive thinking, worry, detailing, incessant self-talk, "stuck record" rumination, and other thought disorders of the adult child sap intellectual capacities.

Rules and roles in our families express the distorted belief systems which adult children construct about themselves and all reality around them. Speaking one's own reality involves constructing piece by piece a new belief system out of which new feelings and new behavior can arise.

This renewing of the mind then will involve learning healthy family rules, healthy roles, and healthy communication patterns. "The truth" to be spoken, the new reality to be learned surfaces significantly in the succeeding features of the discipleship-recovery journey outlined by Paul here in 4:25–5:2 of Ephesians. It will involve learning who we actually are and who God and others are when viewed with decreasing distortion through increasingly clear lenses. David Seamands borrows a Pauline expression to tenderly picture this learning process as "putting away childish things."[9]

Recovery Is for Everyone

The church languishes from the trivialization of "discipleship" into a few selected disciplines of devotion (which in themselves are not to be depreciated) and of learning various communities' particular ethos. Blindness in the church to the lethal nature of "doing and being" patterns that have become accepted as "normal" or unavoidable inhibits appropriation of the gospel's transforming dynamic. What a tragedy.

Discipleship as recovery claims that these issues of putting away the lie and speaking the truth are for everyone, not just for alcoholics, drug addicts, codependents, or other obviously injured souls. The separation of "normal" persons from these populations with recognized problems is more a matter of degree than kind. All disciples of Jesus would be well advised to approach their journey informed by the sort of candid survey of their heritage and their present relationships outlined here.

Speak the Truth

The discipleship-recovery journey from delusion to disclosure is not simply about identifying falsehood and learning the truth. The journey entails *speaking* the truth. This means coming to trust God and others sufficiently, unmasking the lie, and coming to believe the truth sufficiently that one will risk speaking that truth to others. This acknowledges that as we confess our sins to one another we experience healing (James 5:16) and gives at least one specific to the process by which the church builds itself up in love (Eph. 4:16).

This means being done with those games in which I speak something other than the truth—blaming or placating or distracting or manipulating or bullying or fogging. It involves setting aside those rules which perpetuate falsehood—rules forbidding question or comment, rules insisting we talk about things as they should be instead of as they are. Speaking this truth implies confession of need—the need of the one hurt and that of the one who has also hurt others. Speaking the truth goes beyond "You say I have abandoned you" to "In spite of myself, I have abandoned my little ones, and I am deeply sorry." Steps four and five of the Twelve Steps focus directly on these matters of repudiating the lie, speaking the truth and Christian confession. They call for a "moral inventory."

4. We made a searching and fearless moral inventory of ourselves.
5. Admitted to God, to ourselves, and to another human being the exact nature of our wrongs.

In this process Christian "salvation" and "sanctification" come to bear on real life. Each of the strands of the journey touched in 4:25–5:2 has its part of "the lie" to repudiate. Steps four and five apply to them all.

The Radical Reason: Realities of Human Relationships

"Because we are related to one another like parts of a single, living body" states the radical reason for the two points of instruction. My expanded translation makes clear the picture Paul has in mind as he again picks up the human body language of 4:16.

The reasoning is radical because of its profundity and its distance from typical Christian reasoning. We might have expected the apostle to support his exhortations by appealing to law: "Because falsehood breaks God's law and truth telling keeps Torah." Some might have expected to hear a threat: "Because if you lie, God will punish you; if you speak the truth, God will reward you." But no such lesser reasoning appears. Spiritual formation here stands on ground much higher than concern about breaking the law (though this is no trivial matter) or reward and punishment (though these also are legitimate topics for consideration).

What Paul aims for is an approach to following Jesus in which one's concerns have actually shifted from carefully keeping the law and from self-preservation to authentic, loving relationships with other persons in the name of Christ. In these relationships the law is more than kept; it is fulfilled, to use Jesus' term (Matt. 5:21–48). In these relationships reward and punishment are experienced, but as by-products of a life set on following Jesus and learning to live in love.

The apostle most certainly has in mind his readers' participation in the "body of Christ," the church. But having grounded his argument in the fact of human interrelationship in the church, he has by implication grounded it in the fact of human relationships themselves, wherein they share common ground with the nature of human interaction in the church. We have no evidence to indicate that the *nature* of the impact persons in the faith have upon one another and on others is substantially different from the impact all persons have on each other. Truth-telling universally fosters health. Falsehood universally destroys relationships. Destructive anger universally opens to the demonic. Parasitic relationships are destructive whether within the church or beyond.

This means that the apostle has, by implication, effectively grounded his exhortation in the realities discussed in the creation database. The realities of the human connection itself, in all its breadth, depth, and complexity, undergird the apostle's teaching for us to repudiate the lie and speak the truth.

It means as well that to talk about spiritual matters is here to talk about "personal," psychological matters. Personal, psychological issues are spiritual matters in this book, and in the Bible elsewhere.

Spiritual matters here involve personal, psychological matters. "Learning the truth as it is in Jesus" cannot be separated from the questions of personal growth and recovery considered in this look at the journey from delusion to disclosure. That, among other reasons, is why we are claiming discipleship as recovery.

Questions for Reflection

1. Do I spend more time brooding over things I should have said to people than in actually telling important persons in my life what I do think and feel?

2. Do I bury myself in a flurry of activity in order to avoid coming to terms with the state of my relationships with persons who should be among my closest friends?

3. Do I keep myself anesthetized with sexual activity, drugs, religious fervor, or other things in order not to have to deal with either my pain or the voice of God in my life?

4. Do I refuse to accept sincere compliments about my appearance or behavior, diverting them with apologies or qualifications or talk about God?

5. Do I refuse to listen openly to negative information about myself, avoiding this feedback with a flood of tears or bursts of anger or other defenses?

6. Do I run a nonstop comedy act to cover my pain and loneliness?

7. Am I accepting intolerable behavior in myself or behavior toward me that a year ago I would never have thought I would accept?

8. Do I accept rationalizations of my own behavior that I would not accept from someone responsible to me?

9. Do I allow myself to be used and manipulated without significant protest, for fear of losing a relationship, even if it is a degrading relationship?

10. Do I laugh and smile while talking about experiences I have had that are really not funny at all, but are painful and sad and terrible?

11. Do I spend much time playing roles with people in which I appear to be involved and happy, but am actually a million miles away or fed up with the whole mess?

12. Do I permit myself to tell actual, bald-faced lies in order to protect myself or others or to make points with people who are important to me?

13. Have I ever really thought seriously about the ways human beings were treated in the home I grew up in and the impact that is now having on my ability to relate to God and to others?

7

From Destruction to Dynamic
(Ephesians 4:26–27)

Tears from Nowhere

I had become increasingly aware of a recurring experience. Several songs associated with my childhood, "God Leads His Dear Children Along," "His Eye Is on the Sparrow," and the patriotic hymn, "God Bless America" moved me to tears every time I tried to sing them. Stories or pictures of children being taken advantage of brought similar feelings. The surroundings seemed to make no difference. These songs and pictures would bring me to tears without fail.

About this time I heard an interview with a minister from D. C. who described a similar experience. He called it "disassociated emotion" and explained how feelings from painful childhood experiences can become separated in the mind from the events that caused them. Set loose from their moorings, sometimes they attach to other items in our memory and are then triggered by music, smells, tastes, or other aspects associated with these new "anchors." "Disassociated emotions," he opined, flag reservoirs of potent feelings of which one is not aware and with which one has not adequately come to terms. I couldn't think of any childhood experiences sufficiently painful to account for my tears. The encounter left questions I couldn't answer.

I was again becoming aware of great loads of anger occupying my attention. Most of the anger I could tag was unfortunately directed at my wife and various features of our life together that continued to frustrate me. The agendas I had vowed to let go in my '79 "walkout" had obviously not been "let go" in any satisfactory way. Those things mattered far too much to me to just "live and let live." I wondered if *these* feelings were the ones driving my tears. I couldn't really see where or how to pursue this.

The Teaching

*Experience anger in such a way
that you stop sinning in the process.
Stop letting the sun go down on your anger,
thus opening the door for demonic destruction (AOT).*

Paul's move from the journey through delusion (v. 25) to the path through destructive anger (vv. 26–27) is striking, in view of the link between anger and the delusion that plagues adult children. Quoting Psalm 4:4, Paul puts two ideas together to form a single, surprising concept: anger without sin. This "hendiadys" ("one idea through two") uses two imperatives: "Be angry;" "stop sinning." These two express the single notion I have translated above, "Experience anger in such a way that you stop sinning in the process."

The construction should not be read as an encouragement to be angry. Some[1] wish to deny any positive construing at all for anger in these verses, in view of the rejection of raging anger in verse 31. But verses 26–27 *assume* anger and refrain from rejecting that anger itself. Instead the writer focuses on the dangers of *unresolved* anger. Verse 31 on the other hand rejects anger linked with violence.

Repudiate "The Lie" about Anger

Bible Context Again

Just as "the truth" to be spoken by disciples of Jesus (v. 25) involves the instruction of 4:26–5:2, so "the lie" to be put aside finds exposition in these verses as well. In addition, the immediately preceding context of our paragraph (4:17–24) assumes the call to follow Jesus (vv. 20–21) carries a call to reject the mind of "the world" and, by implication, the mind of the church wherever the world has captured it (vv. 17–19). Part of the discipleship-recovery journey to redemptive anger will involve confronting the main lies marketed by one's culture regarding anger. Here are some of the most common of those lies about anger.

Angry, Hateful Acts Do Not Affect People Deeply

MTV and TV/cinematic programming present horrendously violent, angry acts as though they matter little. Persons are murdered, assaulted, and abused while those around them suffer minimal trauma, their lives for the most part repaired in fifty minutes or less. Those who dismiss being a "hothead" or a continually "frustrated person" as a simple personality quirk of strictly private concern also peddle this lie. Real life refutes this.

"Angry" Is an Acceptable Lifestyle

Whole subcultures enshrine this lie. Here are some anger icons of our culture: Redneck "good old boys" who would as soon shoot out your tires as run you off the road; punk rockers whose "in your face" music booms anger; Fonzie types whose "bug off buster" sneers match their "don't tread on me" posture. Played equally well by females, these culture roles say the life of continual, omni-directional anger is OK. That's a lie.

Violence Solves Problems

Rambo life is not real life. Wholesale destruction and macho violence solve problems only in the movies. Disciplined use of force by the state may be necessary to maintain order in society. But wreaking havoc on a family or village or country solves nothing. It misrepresents the sort of behavior appropriate with anger and in any case is certainly no model for personal behavior.

Venting Anger Resolves Anger

It may well prove necessary to express one's anger in some form in order to resolve it. But simply venting anger, either at the persons or situations producing one's anger or at other parties, will not in itself resolve anger.

Anger Must Lead to Irrational, Harmful Behavior

Persons often think of being angry as being out of control, acting irrationally and/or violently. Talk of being "mad" as opposed to being "angry" expresses this idea. This lie confuses the feeling of anger with the behavior used to express that feeling, and associates that feeling only with destructive behavior. The truth is something else.

Holy, Loving Persons Do Not Become Angry

Both the world and the church share this misconception which misunderstands human beings as God made them. It substitutes romantic notions of love for the robust love Jesus lived. The presence of anger in the Holy One Himself refutes this lie.

Now none of this constitutes a plea for Christians to live angrily. We begin by attending to these falsehoods because here as elsewhere telling the truth as it is in Jesus involves repudiating the lie.

Spot Unresolved Anger as a Door for the Demonic

"Stop letting the sun go down on your anger, thus opening the door for demonic destruction" (vv. 26–27) reveals Paul's specific concern here: unresolved anger. He warns that anger carried and nursed gives the Devil a particularly advantageous place to enter human relationships.

Learn the Many Faces of Anger

Some believers prematurely pass over Scripture's teaching on anger. They underestimate or miss the role of anger in their lives because they do not recognize its many faces.

Three foreboding insights from the creation data relate here. First, among the feelings generated by the tragedy of childhood abandonment, intense anger stands near the core. Second, the twisted rules of the child's family often prevent resolution of that anger. Third, that unresolved, invalidated anger is released like dripping cyanide into the child's system. It poisons body and mind under many disguises over decades unless it is resolved.[2] Discipleship-recovery entails identifying the anger at work in our lives under various disguises.

Depression-Despair. Depression can stem from many causes, physical or environmental. Depression can signal the healthy grief of giving up beloved persons or things.[3] So one must resist over-simplification here. Long lasting, major depression will most likely require medical intervention, no matter what its causes are. Even so, it is also true that depression presents one of the most common disguises of unresolved anger. It is anger turned back on oneself.[4] Closely akin to this despair is the feeling of anger now as an intense, nearly insufferable pain in one's soul.

Doubt. If depression is anger turned against oneself, doubt often amounts to anger turned against God. Of course not all doubt springs from unresolved anger. The nature of the cosmos and of human history prompt legitimate questions regarding God. But doubt can represent anger. Ann's question to my tale of God's absence and my nagging doubt was so perceptive: "At whom are you angry?"

Passive Aggression. "Passive" aggression describes aggression veiled by a veneer of social acceptability. Passive aggression attacks in such a way that we either do not clearly recognize the assault or do not know whether to confront it or let it go—again. Habitual lateness, obnoxious "habits," sarcasm, humor at another's expense, insults, overspending, "accidents," "forgetting" matters important to a spouse or friend, and many other sorts of behavior enter the picture here as ways of attacking and discounting others. They are anger in disguise.

Compulsive, Addictive Behavior. The whole range of addictions are actually feeling disorders. They represent ways of coping with core shame and the feelings associated with abandonment, including anger. Because of the prominent place of strong, deep-seated anger among the feelings loosed in the psyches of adult children, their behaviors are to be considered, among other things, faces of anger.

As we have seen, in addition to these "disguises of unresolved anger" which often mask its toxic presence, the more obvious faces of resentment, rage, and hostility signal equally destructive forces at work. These verses call the disciple to also come to terms with them in Jesus' name.

Heed Paul's Strong Warning about the Demonic

The Devil perpetuates delusion (John 8:44) and self-destruction, loss of the capacity to think and speak for oneself, alienation from self, others and God (Mark 5:1–17). The Devil is the adversary of all attempts to actualize the destiny God ordains for His creatures (Eph. 6:11). Our creation resource emphasized just how potent Paul's warning proves to be. In Satir's experience resolution of anger constituted one of the two critical issues to be addressed in family health.[5] Persons nursing resentment unwittingly perpetuate a spiral of misery. The disguised anger just cataloged impairs and even destroys human relationships, reduces productivity, and lowers quality of life.

Unresolved anger takes a steady toll on one's physical health. Anger suppressed "does not dissipate," Firestone warns, "but retains a bodily component." Conscious awareness of the pain is repressed or forgotten, emerging only in disguises like those above. But the forgotten anger continues to inflict damage across a broad front. It finds symbolic expression in the "neurotic and self-destructive behavior" described by the addiction/compulsions and codependent relationships. But it also, as though "stored in layers in the body," causes "tension and psychosomatic illnesses as well as depression and anxiety."[6] Our muscles live tensed up, "on alert;" our bodies get sick.

So we pay a terrible personal, relational, and physical price for anger unleashed in our system, whether we know of it or not. No wonder Paul warned at this particular point that in carrying anger we give place to the Devil.[7]

Commit Yourself to Resolve Your Anger

Beyond "Justification" of Anger

Sounds simple. It really does not matter when or how one came to be angry. The question now is what one will do with that anger. The question is not whether one was justified in one's anger, but whether one will allow God to help resolve that anger. The church's frequent awkwardness regarding anger complicates this journey considerably for many. Adult children experience even more hurdles. They often hit adulthood without much feeling, numbed from their families' "affective anesthesia."[8] For all disciples the project requires intentional pursuit of holy love.

Own Your Anger

"Owning" your anger first means walking the road from delusion to disclosure here too! We repudiate falsehood and speak the truth with regard to anger and its place in our lives. For some this will mean confronting and acknowledging the obvious signs of the angry life and nursed resentment. They are angry, and they know it. But they have somehow thought it didn't matter or had become accustomed to living on edge.

For others owning anger will first mean discovering their anger and learning about its manifestations in their lives. These persons will have to uncover the anger buried beneath a cover of chronic ailments, sneering behind one of its many disguises, and providing fuel for their compulsive, addictive ways. This journey will almost surely be part of their larger project of reclaiming all their emotions— including their anger—and learning really to "feel feelings" again.

Give Your Anger to God

Giving your anger to God does not mean getting rid of our *capacity* for anger or surrendering *responsibility* for our anger. It rather involves owning that anger as a creation endowment meant to serve your needs and bring glory to God. Just as God without the capacity for anger would not be the God and Father of our Lord Jesus, so human beings without anger are not the creatures God planned them to be. Unlike Spock of *Star Trek* fame, we are not Vulcans. We come equipped with anger straight from the "Manufacturer."

Central here is Paul's concept of offering our entire selves "as a living sacrifice" to God (Rom. 12:1). We may picture ourselves taking in our hands the precious gift God Himself has given us and placing it on His altar, offering it to Him for His purifying and His blessing. The miracle of the transaction is that the sacrifice lives! God places the gift offered Him back in our hands as part of the renewing of our mind and equipping for His service (Rom. 12:1–3).

Healing, Redirection, and Forgiveness

Giving your anger to God thus involves "healing for damaged emotions," as David Seamands' book title puts it. The confrontations, discoveries, and learning, and the ownership and surrender just discussed describe part of that healing. But health means not simply the absence of illness but the presence of vitality. So here healing also involves redirection, development of new patterns of experiencing anger.

The discipleship-recovery process of learning new ways touches several different agendas in the journey mapped by the Apostle Paul in 4:25–5:2. Focusing simply on anger as though it were a phenomenon disconnected from other facets of one's life bears small promise. So a good part of the resolution of our anger hinges on insight and obedience to Christ in these other areas.

Expressing Anger Redemptively

Wynne discovered "pseudo-mutuality" and "pseudo-hostility" in troubled families.[9] *Both* masked the real splits, blurred the real problems, and blocked real resolution of conflict with their superficiality. Learning to express anger appropriately moves beyond such "pseudo-hostilities" or truces and seeks to express anger candidly and clearly, but redemptively.

Bradshaw's "fair fighting rules" chart just one practical course for experiencing anger without sin and for "learning to express anger appropriately."[10]

1. Be assertive (self-valuing) rather than aggressive (get the other person no matter what the cost).

2. Stay in the now. Avoid scorekeeping.

3. Avoid lecturing and stay with concrete, specific behavioral detail.

4. Avoid judgment ["you" messages]. Stay with self-responsible "I" messages.

5. Honesty needs to be rigorous. Go for accuracy, rather than agreement or perfection.

6. Don't argue about details, e.g., "You were twenty minutes late;" "No, I was only thirteen minutes late."

7. Don't assign blame.

8. Use active listening. Repeat to the other person what you heard them say. Get their agreement about what you heard them say before responding.

9. Fight about one thing at a time.

10. Unless you are being *abused*, hang in there. This is especially important. Go for a solution rather than being right.

Persons accustomed to living the disguises of anger or harboring resentment will find that these suggestions open an entirely untried way, a discipleship-recovery way.

Reject Cheap Forgiveness, but Do Forgive

Resolving anger involves finding forgiveness—for oneself and others. Giving one's anger to God implies this. Anger of course arises from the feeling that one has been abandoned, assaulted, discounted, or otherwise abused. But as most adult children come to see, the victim often becomes a victimizer. Persons expressing their pain and anger through addictive-compulsive, codependent thinking and behavior invariably wind up violating others in their anger, whether it is covert or overt. When one grasps this debt to others and God, the only recourse is to ask for forgiveness. Awareness of our own need for forgiveness can help in granting forgiveness to others.

Authentic forgiveness is the target here. Cheap forgiveness is more confusion than forgiveness. Sincere disciples of Jesus, ironically, are particularly susceptible to this trap. Not only the church's uneasiness with open anger but also their own sincere desire to follow their Master's pattern of forgiveness draws them into this. "Cheap forgiveness" describes forgiveness that does not count the cost. This means forgiveness that either does not take seriously enough the damage actually inflicted on one's person or does not reckon sufficiently with the challenge of really forfeiting the "right" to revenge. And so we must stop mistaking the trivializing of wrongs with forgiveness.

Forgiving does mean letting the other person off the hook—really, literally, deeply, fully—for wrongs squarely faced. Forgiveness means relinquishing the right to retaliate. We place these matters in the hands of God, who has promised one day to make moral sense of all history—including our own. So we might support forgiveness by picturing ourselves taking our "moral ledger book" in our hands, placing it as our gift on the altar, and leaving the keeping of accounts to God.

Seek Reconciliation, If Possible

The resolution of anger and forgiveness surely relates to reconciliation, but they are not the same thing. Discovering, identifying, owning, and relinquishing anger transpire within the angry one. As a matter of fact, adult children (and others) often find themselves consumed with anger when the individual(s) with whom they are angry remain oblivious to the fact or are entirely out of the picture, even dead. These other parties sense no rupture in relationships, even though the quality of the relationship may be seriously deficient. They would not understand "reconciliation," should it be sought.

Coming to terms with such persons may include disclosing to them, where possible, one's own feelings and unveiling one's own alienation from them, quite apart from their perceptions. It may include leveling with them concerning abuse perpetrated upon oneself as a child or other wrongs done to oneself. Such disclosures could serve to register objection as an adult to matters about which one could do nothing as a child. They might make "public," at least between two parties (and perhaps with others also involved), what was "hidden" between them. They may also prevent further abuse to others.

These disclosures would intend to prepare the way for announcing forgiveness as well. Just as Gerald Ford's pardon of Richard Nixon not only granted official forgiveness, but also publicly acknowledged crimes Mr. Nixon himself never candidly admitted, so such granting of forgiveness speaks both the desire for reconciliation *and* the recognition of sin at the same time. These sorts of transactions carry their own risks. Some persons will hear this forgiveness as insight, and receive it as an invitation to grow. Others may hear it as an accusation against which they must defend themselves, taking the offensive and doing further damage.

We have responsibility for only one side of such reconciliations—our own, since we literally cannot make others feel or do anything. But that responsibility we do have. We seek reconciliation by acknowledging *our* anger and *our* wrong, by announcing and requesting forgiveness and declaring our commitment to restoration of fellowship. Such reconciling overtures shine like bright light against the dark background of a litigious, retaliatory world.

Steps eight and nine of the Twelve Steps speak to the topic of reconciliation and the closely related idea of restitution. They say:

8. We made a list of all persons we had harmed, and became *willing* to make amends to them all [emphasis mine].

9. We made direct amends to such people wherever possible, except when to do so would injure them or others.

Reconciliation constitutes part of "making amends." But "making amends" reminds us that part of reconciliation will often be restitution, making material restitution for damage inflicted. And step nine wisely raises the idea that sometimes reconciliation/making amends will cause more harm than good, as we noted above, and should not in those cases be pursued.

"Seek reconciliation, *if possible*," also recognizes that some reconciliation, particularly with abusive persons who will not confront their own destructive behavior, may not be possible or even advisable. The risk of continuing abuse or bodily harm to ourselves or others for whom we are responsible may mean that re-establishment of relationships cannot occur. One may be able to resolve one's own anger but not be able to resume life under the same roof or continue in close association with another. Conflicting moral responsibilities in such cases make it impossible to predict in each specific case what course will best embody holy love.

The disciple lives not only with the Master's example of recon-ciliation (e.g., with Peter who denied Him, Mark 14:26–31, 66–72; 16:7; John 21:15–19) but also with His example of exposing and confronting evil (Mark 7:6–16; 11:15–19; 12:1–11; cf. Eph. 5:11). On the one side stands the difficult opportunity to witness to the love of Christ through freely and knowingly submitting oneself to suffering and abuse—a choice one cannot make for one's children or one's spouse. On the other stands the responsibility to withstand evil and resist injustice, including injustice done to oneself. Providing support and counsel for these sorts of decisions gives one specific item of content to the idea of the church building itself up in love (Eph. 4:16).

Finally, "seek reconciliation, *if possible*," recognizes that, unlike forgiveness, reconciliation is a two-way street. I can forgive at any time, whether another party responds appropriately or even knows of that forgiveness. Reconciliation, on the other hand, means that both parties, not just one, accept the truth about themselves and the ruptured relationship.[11] We have responsibility for *our* accept-ance of the truth. We cannot make others do the same.

Follow Jesus as Master in Holy Anger, Too!

Paul views this discipleship-recovery journey as living "the truth as it is in Jesus" (4:21). This leads us to ask about Jesus' model of experiencing anger. Discipleship, we recall, is learning by fol-lowing Him! Not only so but, insofar as Jesus reveals God, Jesus' anger is God's anger as well! So we have further reason to pursue His model, for we are called to be "imitators of God" (5:1).

When we turn to Paul's letters looking for guidance as to what particular episodes in the life of Jesus he might have named, had we asked him about Jesus' anger, we draw a surprising blank. Paul no doubt knew many stories about Jesus' life that we now find in our gospels, stories carrying pictures of Jesus' behavior and spirit and the content of His teaching.[12] These treasured stories were so carefully crafted, preserved, and transmitted as to be considered "tradition" (1 Cor. 15:1). But Paul tells us very little else about the life of Jesus. So in this case we must look to the Gospels for clues to following Jesus' anger. We will use Mark.

Be Angry at the Things That Anger Jesus

Mark chooses to place pictures of anger in Jesus' life at important junctures in his presentation of the good news of Jesus (Mark 3:1–6; 10:13–16; 11:11–19). While these episodes surely do not exhaust such information from Jesus' life, they do give significant direction as to the sorts of things about which Jesus felt anger.

Religious Tradition over Healing of Persons (Mark 3:1–6). The snapshot comes from Jesus' experience on a Sabbath day in a synagogue. Three parties fill the picture: Jesus, a man with a crippled hand, and people watching to see whether He would heal the man on the Sabbath. God's instruction through Moses commanded the "hallowing" of the Sabbath (i.e., specifically setting it aside as God's day) by refraining from work (Ex. 20:8–11). By Jesus' time, some devout Jews had developed elaborate traditional laws of their own designed to define more carefully what constituted "work" and also to safeguard the keeping of God's command.

Jesus leveled a three-pronged critique at this approach. First, in spite of the good intentions of many Pharisees, it tended to produce a sort of artificial "godliness" where one's lips "talked the talk," but one's heart was far from God's heart (Mark 7:6–8). Second, it tended to produce persons who could ignore the Lawgiver's intent, while technically keeping the law (Mark 7:9–13). And last, it failed to understand the nature of real inner purity (7:14–23). From the picture in Mark, chapter 3, we know that these things not only grieved Jesus but also angered Him.

In the synagogue, Jesus' questions implied God's priorities differed from these devoutly religious people. Religious tradition that failed to preserve God's heart for helping persons, for healing, and enhancing life prompted anger in Jesus. And persons who could remain silent, putting the preservation of that tradition over the opportunity for a man to be whole today(!), angered Jesus. Mark called it "hardness of heart" (Mark 3:5).[13] This model of Jesus places the healing and help of persons as a priority over the traditions of any given nation, family, institution, region, or culture.

Abuse of "Little Ones" (Mark 10:13–16). In this picture of Jesus, parents are bringing their children to the famous Teacher for His blessing. For some unstated reason, Jesus' disciples obstruct their path and forbid them to bring these little ones to Jesus. Although we are not given the reason for this particular crowd control, the context of Mark does not lead us to think it noble (cf. Mark 10:35–45). Mark says Jesus was angry when He saw this.

Children in the ancient world counted little, particularly female children. Even in Jewish society, where life had more value than among their pagan neighbors, little children stood at the bottom of the social ladder along with slaves. These little ones, then, represented all the no-clout, no-power people of the world, at the opposite end of the respectability and power from Jesus, the Great Teacher. Itinerant, untutored person that He was, crowds still flocked from all over Syria-Palestine to hear Him and touch Him for healing (Mark 3:7–12).

Seeing what the disciples were doing, Jesus was angry. In this discounting of little persons, this shaming and undercutting of human dignity, Jesus apparently saw persons who would undercut their own colleagues to get power, and even try to use God and His Messiah for their own selfish ends (Mark 10:35 ff.). This angered Jesus. "Let the children come to me, and stop blocking their way," Jesus commanded (Mark 10:14 AOT).

Religion as Route to Power and Wealth (Mark 11:15–19). The final picture of Jesus' anger shows His response to the use of religious position and structures to gain wealth and power. Confronting the lucrative enterprises thriving in the Jerusalem Temple to "assist" worshipers, Jesus was angry. These services originated in the well-intentioned attempt to help pilgrims from afar have suitable sacrifices for worship. By Jesus' day this "service" had grown to a lucrative and corrupt operation, extending the power of wealthy clergy in Jerusalem. Jesus would have none of this prostitution of the structures of institutional faith. In a move that probably cost Him His life, He evicted these proprietors and their customers and reaffirmed the Temple as a place for prayer.

Do the Kinds of Things Jesus Did in His Anger

Here comes the surprise for persons who have bought the lie that "angry" equals out-of-control behavior. Here we see how anger actually serves as a dynamic. Anger impels loving action, motivates behavior that redeems and elevates human beings instead of discounting and destroying them. Look at the directions Jesus takes, if we follow Him.

Heal (Mark 3:5). In the synagogue, saddened to the core and angered by the insensitivity of these "worshipers" to human hurt and God's heart for the hurting, Jesus healed a man. His anger motivated Him to rock the boat, to risk moving contrary to accepted traditions of godliness in order to heal human hurt.

Intervene on Behalf of "Little Ones" (Mark 10:13–16). On the road, confronted with the patronizing behavior of His disciples toward the little ones, He stepped in, intervening on their behalf and that of their parents. This initiative He need not have taken. Jesus' anger prompted intervention, both to help these little ones and to rebuke their abusers.

Embrace and Bless the "Little Ones" (Mark 10:13–16). And look at this "angry Man" in action! The parents came for a blessing, hoping the Rabbi would perhaps place His hand on their heads and pronounce a blessing. Jesus not only blessed these little ones; Mark emphasizes that Jesus "enfolded them in his arms" (Mark 10:16).[14] He affirmed them not only in word but also with affection and touch. In His anger He spoke love with His body to these little ones.

Commit to Long-Term Help for Offenders (Mark 10). What about the disciples? This failure on their part did not derail Jesus' long-term commitment to teach them. Without minimizing the seriousness of their failure, He immediately moved on, communicating the assumption that they could and would be different. His anger only strengthened His resolve to help these disciples understand what it actually would mean to follow Him (10:14–15).

Act Vigorously to Expel and Restrain Evil (Mark 11:11–19). For the extortioners and embezzlers in the Temple, Jesus also gave instruction. But first He forcefully intervened to expel the evil He saw and restrain its impact. Persons on the discipleship-recovery journey may well encounter evil of this sort. Here their anger may be a critical energizer in moving them to follow the Master. This anger, like that with the children or the people in the synagogue, remains tied to the compassion and love of Jesus. Love and anger are inextricably intertwined in the heart of persons whose feelings, anger and all, are redeemed by the grace of God and His mind-renewing Spirit.

This is at least part of the discipleship-recovery journey *From Destruction to Dynamic.*

Questions for Reflection

1. Do I live as though I believe the lie that holy, loving people really don't experience anger?

2. Do I have a growing list of persons from whom I am alienated or with whom I have broken relationships?

3. Do I nurse my anger, rehearsing over and over how I have been offended, or am I ready to surrender that anger to Messiah Jesus?

4. Do I simply look for occasions to vent my anger and express my anger, or am I really interested in resolving the anger I carry?

5. Am I ready to give up retaliation, attack, and retribution in order to have God's true Shalom—serenity and health of body, mind, and spirit?

6. Do I minimize the anger and hurt I feel and offer cheap grace to people without really owning and naming my anger and, therefore, without really taking it in hand so as to release it to God?

7. Have I ever seriously thought what might account for the fact that I exhibit so many of the masks of anger, why I am so self-destructive or abusive of others?

8. Do I stand limp and unfeeling in the presence of sin and injustice to others and myself that should anger me and impel me to holy action?

9. Have I romanticized Jesus to the point that I have trivialized His anger and thereby lost the opportunity to follow Him in my anger?

10. Am I trying all by myself to handle my anger-producing experiences, or have I asked some "family of choice" to be channels of God's grace to help me find resolution to my anger and, if possible, reconciliation with others?

From Parasite to Partner

(Ephesians 4:28)

One Parasite's Power Struggle

"**P**ower struggle," she said. It was around the spring of 1984. We had engaged Reverend Edna Hoover to teach about family life for our church's community adult education venture. She announced she would teach about "family systems," and I looked forward to this friend's good teaching. Toward the end of the week, when she had sketched the ways families grow and interact like sensitive ecosystems, I pulled her aside for a question. "What does it mean when one member of a couple is always late?" I asked.

I'm not sure why this particular item of punctuality surfaced when I had the opportunity to "get help," though it was one of my big ticket grievances. It made no difference what our obligations were, how serious they were, or how long we had to get ready, Ede would inevitably be late. In meeting her own obligations and appointments she seemed punctual enough. But if I was involved, there was no doubt what to expect. We would all be late. So, what did that mean?

Habitual lateness reflected a power struggle, Edna thought. She saw it as guerrilla warfare used by a marriage partner who felt disempowered and abused. Stripped of power and ability to influence their own situation meaningfully, they resorted to such ways of retaining at least some control of their lives.

A "power struggle"? Why would Ede feel disempowered? Warfare? Is that what we had? What did this mean? Edna had opened a significant door, but several years would pass before I would walk through it. Focused on my own grievances, I had become blind to the staggering toll my anger was exacting from my wife and children. That my wife was under assault at my hands, overpowered by me in any way would never have occurred to me.

As a matter of fact, we both engaged in pretty serious guerrilla tactics. For such "parasitic" relationships, Ephesians 4:28 speaks hope.

The Teaching

Let the one who stole steal no more,
but let him work hard, doing good with his own hands,
that he may have something to share with the one in need
(AOT).

Paul charts the discipleship-recovery journey from "parasite to partner" with a striking, three-part plan much like his reasoning for the journey from delusion to disclosure in verse 25. This part of the journey, like the other parts, begins with "putting away the lie" with regard to parasitic life—or it does not begin at all. Identify and call a halt to the life of theft, he urges.

But ceasing sin constitutes only half the task. Forging the life of holy love remains the central point of this instruction in discipleship-recovery, as it does in all other instructions. So the apostle encourages predators, among whom we are all to be numbered at one time or another, to take responsibility for themselves and their own resources. Not only so, but they are to take charge of themselves in such ways that they actually effect good. This character renovation involves the transformation of life habits from parasite to partner.

The depth of the character transformation envisioned appears in the underlying reason, as in 4:25. That reason, stated this time in terms of a goal ("So then . . ."), pictures erstwhile thieves now concerned about the needs of others and acting to meet those needs. Parasites become partners! Amazing!

Identify and Stop Parasitic Relationships

This recovery teaching aims to transform life habit. Moving beyond God's forgiveness for specific acts of theft, it addresses human relationships characterized by theft. The venerable KJV's translation, "Let him that stole steal no more," brings this out, translating well a construction that identifies a particular person by characteristic behavior and implying this former behavior now comes to a halt.[1]

Thieves live off the resources of other persons. Thus the "theft life" is characterized by relationships with other people that are parasitic. "Parasite" names an organism or plant that lives at the expense of another plant or organism, leaching the life resources from it. Grim visions of truly ugly parasites like the Haitian lung-worm or intestinal tapeworms and roundworms leap to mind. As we shall see, in many cases we might better think of "lovely" parasites, like Spanish moss or kudzu or even poison ivy. Their beauty from a distance disguises the damage being done to the trees on which they live and, in the case of poison ivy, the nasty effects of touching that lush plant. In either case, the picture is clear: life at the expense of another.

Identify Parasite Relationships

Bringing the parasitic life to a halt assumes "putting away the lie" in this part of our lives as in others. Actual property theft comes quickly to mind as the common picture of "the one who steals"—thieves, bank robbers, and the like. And rightly so. But further investigation regarding dysfunctional families often quickly uncovers actual property theft "right here in River City," even in "good Christian families."

Property Parasites. Savings and loan embezzlers, con artists we know. And this verse aims at such persons, for the gospel does not aim simply to make "good" people better, but speaks hope to persons most would agree are parasites. (Remember

Paul's words to the Corinthians regarding "thieves" and other sinners: "And such were some of you," 1 Cor. 6:11 KJV.) But living as a financial parasite often occurs in ostensibly more benign ways in adult children, codependents, and others plagued by addictive, compulsive behavior.

Persons who spend the family's resources without concern for its impact on the other members of the family exhibit serious parasitic behavior. Dysfunctional families often experience the drain of one or more persons who buy to binge, or to compensate for their own sense of inadequacy, or to attack, or get leverage on others. They buy clothes, food, cars, property, trinkets—anything—usually items not really needed and which the family cannot afford. This squandering of the family's financial resources can go on only as the rest of the family somehow absorbs the cost of the assault. Even in cases where the family's ability to "afford" the items is not a problem, their right to enter freely into the family's decisions as to how its resources will be used is taken from them. These relationships can only be characterized as parasitic.

Emotional and Spiritual Parasites. Emotional parasites drain emotional and spiritual energy from those around them and can only continue as these persons absorb the cost of their behavior. All toxic communication patterns carry these sorts of parasitic relationships. Persons who habitually gripe, criticize, browbeat, nag, curse, shout, sass, spit, lie, and otherwise poison their environment, leach life from those around them as surely as the Haitian lungworm does from its "hosts."

Enmeshed persons, who smother others with affection, who control and overdirect them, sap energy from these persons. Codependents, who confuse love with pity and continually manipulate others into "needy" positions so they can rescue them, do the same. Guilt dumpers are emotional and spiritual parasites. They make those around them responsible for their own blunders. They can transform virtually any item into an issue of moral responsibility for which others stand in debt to them. Bigoted persons, who perpetuate ethnic, religious, racial, gender, or other prejudice, assailing the dignity and worth of others around them on the basis of race, color, sex, ethnic identity, or other bases, draw the emotional life blood from others.

Sexual Parasites. One may think first of forceful sexual abuse here: rape, incest, molestation. And rightly so. We must not think such tragedies as foreign to the discipleship-recovery journey. Sexual abuse stands among the shocking "secrets" of too many Christian homes, if recent reports are anywhere near correct. Paul's encouraging word to the Corinthians speaks hope here too. Listing "fornicators . . . adulterers, male prostitutes, sodomites," Paul continues, "And this is what some of you *used to be.* But you were washed, you were sanctified, you were justified in the name of the Lord Jesus Christ and in the Spirit of our God" (1 Cor. 6:9–11 NRSV, emphasis added; cf. "You *were* of the darkness," Eph. 5:8 AOT).

But sexual abuse comes in both overt *and* covert forms. Inappropriate sexual talking in front of children, invading children's privacy, enabling children to witness adult sexual activity, exposing children to nudity after they become aware of adult body parts—these constitute covert sexual abuse. Cross-generational bonding that establishes the child as a surrogate spouse and easily moves to romantic or sexual manifestations represents a form of this covert sexual abuse.

All these various relationships prove parasitic, whether the participants know it or not. If the victims are aware of what is going on, they must decide whether to absorb the impact or fend it off, and then invest the energy in doing one or the other. The fact that one may be ignorant of this process does not lessen the toll.

Parasites and "Boundary" Issues

"I felt invaded!" persons often confess after being robbed—even if the robbery occurred during their absence! When they walk into their home to find valuables gone and belongings strewn around, the sense of being invaded sometimes even overshadows the actual dollar value of the loss. This sense of invasion exposes a basic issue involved in the parasitic life, the issue of boundaries. Theft is an obvious invasion of someone's boundary. But the whole range of parasitic relationships presents equally potent boundary violations.

Boundaries mark the physical and psychological "space" each of us assumes and needs in healthy relationships. The distance acceptable between individuals engaged in a friendly, face-to-face conversation is but one of many expressions of this sense of "space."[2] Pia Mellody explains boundary systems as "invisible and symbolic 'fences'" with three purposes:

- To keep people from coming into our space and abusing us,
- To keep us from going into the space of others and abusing them, and
- To give each of us a way to embody our sense of "who we are."[3]

External and internal boundaries make up our boundary system. Mellody describes our external boundaries as allowing us "to choose our distance from other people" and enabling us "to give or refuse permission for them to touch us." At the same time they similarly protect others from us. She divides our external boundaries into physical and sexual boundaries. Our internal boundaries, she says, "protect our thinking, feeling, and behavior and keep them functional."[4] It is precisely these internal boundaries which enable us to "take responsibility for our thinking, feelings, and behavior and keep them separate from that of others." This taking charge of oneself has two critical results. It enables us to

- Stop blaming others for what we think, feel, and do, and
- Stop taking responsibility for the thoughts, feelings, and behaviors of others.

Internal boundaries, then, allow us to take responsibility for ourselves. They let us stop rationalizing our invasion of other persons' physical and psychological space, stop allowing others to invade our own space, and stop manipulating and controlling those around us.

It is not difficult to see how the issue of parasitic relationships is at heart a matter of boundaries.

Codependents and Addicts as Parasites

Functional boundaries allow nurturing and intimate relationships with others. They are strong but flexible and under the control of the person to whom they belong. Thieves and parasites show damaged boundaries. They construct relationships with other persons which violate the boundaries of these persons and often of themselves as well.

The creation database showed one of the chief symptoms of codependency to be "difficulty setting functional boundaries."[5] Persons who grew up in addicted or otherwise dysfunctional families regularly grow up with impaired boundaries, an almost inevitable result of the breach of their own boundaries experienced in childhood. In these families, you may recall, children serve to meet their parents' needs. And, as Middleton-Moz explains, "the crucial developing boundary between the 'me' and 'not me' . . . will suffer as a result."[6]

Thus, adult children almost inevitably wind up living in some way as parasites. They either overtly assault family members with the socially more odious addictions, or they covertly drain them through codependent relationships or the more socially acceptable addictions. The addictive nature of even these parasitic ways can be seen, for example, in such cases as those where a person keeps buying unwanted "gifts" for his spouse. In spite of the fact that the spouse protests the gifts, and in spite of the fact that the budget cannot stand more "gifts," the "giving" continues. The need of the giver not the receiver obviously prompts these "gifts." This "gift giving" is really passive aggression. Other forms of "helping when it's not good" are in the genre of behavior by which Christian parents pass core shame to their offspring.[7] Garth Wood calls this unnecessary helping "the cruelty of kindness."[8]

The first installment, then, in the discipleship-recovery journey from parasite to partner is identifying and stopping parasitic relationships. Here, as in the other journeys, much of the power of the teaching rests on not trivializing or overly restricting it to the needs of a few select thieves in the community. Spotting the issues at stake and pursuing the implication of the "theft life" leads easily to the whole range of parasitic relationships involved in the standard life of adult children and codependent persons. Picturing oneself as a parasite and the sorts of relationships easily excused and rationalized by addiction and codependence as parasitic, though painful, may foster insight here.

Take Responsibility for Yourself and Your Own Resources

Real "Self-Help"

"But let him work hard, doing good with his own hands," Paul continues (4:28). Forging the life of holy love entails not simply the cessation of theft but the responsible, redemptive use of one's own resources. This means taking responsibility for *oneself* and the use of one's *own* resources, as "with his *own* hands" emphasizes.

We can scarcely exaggerate the importance of this "taking charge of oneself." Perhaps nowhere in this paragraph does Paul make clearer the principle that runs beneath all biblical theology and all teaching on Christian discipleship and the life of holy love. Whatever we make of the grace of God and the various environmental factors influencing us, we can never make of it the surrender of personal responsibility for our own future and claim either authentic Christian discipleship or good recovery. Whole monographs like Garth Wood's *The Myth of Neurosis: Overcoming the Illness Excuse* emphasize the counterproductive effect of the creation resource when it is used to absolve persons from the responsibility of taking charge of themselves. Equally destructive are understandings of grace and Christian assurance that undermine accountability.

"Work with your own hands" dramatizes this call to take one's life in one's own hands. Surely we have seen enough of Ephesians by now to realize that this represents no jettison of utter dependence on the grace of God and His profound engagement in our lives. No "do-it-yourself" movement, Christian discipleship nevertheless insists on our accountable participation in the journey. It is no downhill coast, but a stiff climb. Scott Peck zeroes in on our point: "We do not become partners to evil by accident. As adults we are not forced by fate to become trapped by an evil power; we set the trap ourselves."[9]

Peck calls for the use of that freedom by grace, and the "unsetting" of the trap for ourselves. Outlining what he considers "the basic set of tools [he calls these 'discipline'] we require to solve life's problems," he includes "acceptance of responsibility" as one of these basics.[10]

This need to take responsibility ultimately for oneself represents the core contention of "self-help" in the recovery movement. Christian critiques of this "self-help" notion as excluding God and selling "works righteousness"[11] often miss the target. It is true that some versions of recovery and "self-help" either explicitly or implicitly reject God or the need for divine help. Or they mistakenly identify "god" with one's own interior resources. But more often than not, "self-help" means simply this very taking charge of oneself and leaving behind the life of rationalization of oneself and manipulation of others. It *assumes* the help not only of a community but of God as well. Whatever the case, Paul's point is clear.

Break Predatory and Codependent Relationships

The teaching strikes to the heart of the needs of adult children and codependents in two ways. First, it asks them to take responsibility for themselves and their own resources, effecting good in the process. Second, it asks them to choose behaviors that embody the "partner" relationships. Adult children tend either to be super irresponsible, caring for no resources (their own or others), or super responsible, caring inordinately for others to the detriment of themselves and ultimately the others as well. Thus they tend to become either addictive predators and wasters on the one hand, or rescuers, martyrs, and messiahs on the other. Neither of these sick approaches expresses holy love.

A two-pronged attack emerges. First, the disciple must stop rationalizing his or her predatory ways. Second, the disciple must stop taking responsibility for the thinking, feeling, doing of other persons for which he or she is not responsible. On the one hand, addictive-compulsive modes of relating come under scrutiny. On the other, the codependent's chief trap of "otheration"—being addicted to and directed by others—is addressed.

This redirection thus leads disciples straight to two of the core symptoms of codependents, according to Mellody: 1) difficulty setting functional boundaries, and 2) confusion of wants and needs.[12] Regarding difficulty setting functional boundaries, taking responsibility for themselves calls adult children to build boundaries that are intact for both their own welfare *and* the protection of those around them.

Thus adult children confuse "responsibility to others" in two contradictory directions, the one most destructive of others, the other most destructive of themselves. Both are addressed by the development of healthy boundaries. On the one hand, they often disregard the person and property of others. Discipleship-recovery here means learning legitimate responsibility to others that arises from acting responsibly oneself, learning to respect others and their boundaries, so as to stop predatory ways. On the other hand, they feel *over*-responsible for others, taking responsibility that they cannot and should not shoulder. This often entails parasitic relationships of a more covert nature that undercuts their own ability to care for themselves and legitimately offer help to others. Discipleship-recovery here builds the ability to care for oneself as a basis for honestly caring for others.

But the redirection also necessitates coming to grips with codependents' deep confusion over needs and wants. As Mellody puts it, codependents have "difficulty acknowledging and meeting [their] own needs and wants."[13] This leads to being either 1) *too* dependent on others, 2) *anti*dependent, 3) "needless and wantless," i.e., not aware of their own needs and wants, or 4) confused in their wants and needs.[14] When these confusions are put together with the impaired or damaged boundaries of adult children, parasitic ways are close at hand. Invading other people's property and person, violating their internal and external boundaries deliberately or unknowingly, can easily become a way of life. Thus when Wilson lists the skills that children of alcoholics will most likely have to learn, since they missed them in childhood, she names "limit-setting" among the three identified.[15] In her "Progression of Recovery Issues" for adult children, beside these boundary issues she puts the issue of "neglecting own needs" and names "realizing I have needs," "identifying needs," and "getting needs met appropriately" as the progression.[16]

Recovery here will be work indeed, for these and other habits of sin are deeply ingrained in us by the time we get around to taking up the discipleship-recovery journey. And the needs and pains that fuel them are profoundly imprinted upon our adult child, as we have seen. Paul's choice of words which highlight the "hard work" (KVJ, "labor") is directly to the point. He exhorts the thief to move from predatory ways to hard, manual labor—"hard work with the hands." This primary meaning gives us the picture. As we have seen, however, the line that separates blatant thievery from the violation of boundaries in dysfunctional families and codependent relationships is much less pronounced than one might have thought. Pursuit of the teaching's implications quickly takes one through the whole territory.

Discipleship Curriculum

This transformation of life pattern involves learning new ways—the ways themselves and their doing. For many persons it means working through a significant discipleship curriculum in which they learn:

- The meaning of boundaries
- The most common manifestations of impaired, damaged, or non-existent boundaries
- The content of healthy boundaries and how they look in operation
- All these learnings as features of growth in grace
- The difference between human wants and needs, for insight into oneself and prioritizing ministry to others
- How to meet needs and satisfy wants in "redemptive" ways, i.e., ways that work "the good"

Melody Beattie offers an exercise in establishing healthy boundaries which exemplifies the sort of learning to be done. Here are boundary-setting affirmations from her *Codependent No More*, with my comments in brackets.[17]

Boundary Affirming Statements

- I will not allow anyone to physically or verbally abuse me. [That is, not without my consent. Authentic self-sacrifice is no pathology. "Sacrificing myself" because I lack the moral courage or inner strength to stand up for myself as a human being is no virtue. Cf. John 13:1–5.]

- I will not knowingly believe or support lies.
- I will not allow chemical abuse in my home.
- I will not allow criminal behavior in my home. [Just how difficult this becomes when the criminal is one's own son, daughter, or spouse surprises many people.]
- I will not rescue people from the consequences of their alcohol abuse or other irresponsible behavior. [Reversing this when you've spent your life invading other people's space by rescuing them and helping them when they should better have helped themselves proves a stout task indeed.]
- I will not finance a person's alcoholism or other irresponsible behavior.
- I will not lie to protect you or me from your alcoholism [or other compulsive, codependent, adult child behavior].
- I will not use my home as a detoxification center for recovering alcoholics.
- If you want to act crazy that's your business, but you can't do it in front of me. Either you leave or I'll walk away. [This is particularly difficult when the "crazy" involves the unhealthy use of religion or toxic forms of "discipling."]
- You can spoil your fun, your day, your life—that's your business—but I won't let you spoil my fun, my day, or my life.

These constitute significant learning in the life of holy love. The very process of establishing, evaluating, and living out these boundaries fosters significant progress in setting aside parasitic ways and working the good with one's own hands.

Take Charge of Your Own Resources to Effect Good

The reach of our own reality presents a good starting measure of our own resources: our bodies, our thoughts, our feelings, our behavior. With these at the very least we may work "with our hands" to effect good. Our resources include all our holdings—material, financial, physical, mental, spiritual, emotional, and relational resources.

Setting boundaries means I don't expend resources I don't have in any of these categories. Part of the erstwhile thief's task is learning to take care of himself or herself and to do so in ways that do not adversely affect others. This "taking care of oneself" amounts to "taking possession of oneself," not a fixation on oneself. One takes possession of oneself in the name of Christ in order to be able authentically to give oneself to others. One cannot really give away what one has not taken in hand.

Thus setting boundaries also means I know with increasing clarity what my resources really are. It means, on the one hand, setting aside grandiose ideas that I can meet everyone's needs. But it also means putting away the adult child's fears that he or she has nothing to work with. It involves seeing the terrific worth of the full range of resources God has placed in every human being's hands. It entails also using these for the glory of God and the good of others, as well as the meeting of one's own needs.

Reach Out to Others Without Losing Your Own Identity

Goal: From Codependent to Interdependent and Beyond

"That she (or he) may have something to share with the one in need" (4:28). As we noted at the outset, Paul concludes this teaching with a radical reason phrased in a purpose statement. To *this* end the journey from parasitic relationships is moving. If codependency generally best describes the pattern of human relationships which prove parasitic, *inter*dependency describes the sort of relationships toward which the discipleship-recovery journey of holy love aims and which it embodies.[18] If inadequate boundaries and confusion of wants and needs describe the particular symptoms of codependence at issue, building intact boundaries and clarifying wants and needs name the tasks germane to the journey to the "partner" life.

Mutuality and complementarity describe the kinds of family and personal relationships envisioned here as at least a preliminary stage of growth in the partnership life. "Simply" rising to "healthy relationships" involves, in Nathan Ackerman's words, a "shared concern for one another's welfare" in meeting the family's needs at five levels: 1) support of self-esteem; 2) cooperation in quest for solutions to conflict; 3) satisfaction of needs; 4) support of needed defenses against anxiety; 5) support for development and creative fulfillment of individual family members.[19]

These sorts of complementary, mutual relationships assume and express healthy personal boundaries. Mellody outlines inadequate boundaries as of four main types.[20]

Some persons have *nonexistent boundaries*—they simply aren't there. These disciples have no protection and experience no real intimacy. Without boundaries they cannot value the boundaries of others and are set up to be offenders. Without boundaries they cannot protect themselves, and they may mistake unlimited access to themselves as intimacy and be open to victimization.

Damaged boundaries have "holes" in them, as Mellody puts it.[21] These people have adequate boundaries except that illness, weariness, stress, or particular stressors like spouse or authority figures render them unable to set boundaries. They have limited protection and impaired intimacy.

Walls *instead of boundaries* provide complete protection but preclude intimacy. Persons build walls with anger, fear, silence, words, and other defenses.

Rebound from walls to "shields down" and back to walls, etc. The anxiety of exposure suffered in the risk of taking down the walls, and the loneliness of isolation behind walls, set up this yo-yo existence which offers neither lasting protection nor intimacy. These impaired boundaries almost inevitably lead to the parasitic life in one way or another.

In contrast to these impaired boundaries the discipleship-recovery journey heads for intact boundaries, where both protection and vulnerability thrive. Unless overpowered by persons of greater physical or emotional strength, persons with intact boundaries have a confidence that they are safe and can protect themselves without throwing up the shields to cut off contact with the outside world. At the same time they are strong enough to allow others into their mental, spiritual, and physical space. Only this sort of vulnerability to real persons opens the possibility of meeting another's needs as they actually are.

"Rooted in Love" Reorientation

"Having something to give to the one in need" names one agenda in the curriculum of comprehending "with all saints what is the breadth and the length and height and depth [of the love of Christ]" and coming to know that love (Eph. 3:18–19). It also describes a whole reorientation of life best described as "rooted and grounded in love" (3:17). The inner strengthening by God's Spirit and the newly transforming presence of God's Messiah in their hearts will issue in precisely the sort of inner reorientation demanded by chapter 4, verse 28. That reorientation in love will open the way for the sort of learning and growing necessary to transform parasites into partners. It provides inner resolve and assurance necessary to stay with the curriculum of spiritual growth provided by life's problems.

Steps six and seven of the Twelve Steps call for actual character transformation.

6. We were entirely ready to have God remove all these defects of character.

7. We humbly asked Him to remove our shortcomings.

"These defects" may begin with the surface behavior of alcoholism and other addictive, codependent behavior. But the "defects of character" run much deeper and reach to "the *core* defect," a whole orientation of self addressed by Paul's prayer and the teaching of discipleship-recovery here.

The "rooted in love" reorientation moves beyond interdependence and mutuality to the will and capacity to minister to the needs of persons who cannot be "interdependent," to the needy who cannot or will not be "mutual." The destiny of holy love envisioned in Ephesians 1:4 has in mind the ability to expend oneself and one's resources for others from healthy boundaries and considered devotion to Christ, not to be driven by one's own unmet needs. Discipleship-recovery cannot stop either with the satisfaction only of one's own needs or the achievement of "mere" mutuality, though these are truly significant.[22]

This new orientation has the parasite-now-become-partner actually interested in the needs of another person in his or her own right and sensitive enough to such persons as to be able to discern their need. This does not perpetuate the "rescuer trap" or the "martyr mire." It leads "rescuers" to separate themselves sufficiently from others so that they can actually see their needs. It calls for rescuers to gain enough clarity about themselves to define themselves first as "well beloved children," and second, as a person who meets the needs of others. "Martyrs" are called away from melodramatic self-sacrifice and the exaggerated self-pity oozing from it. They are led to strength and identity to enable them authentically to sacrifice themselves for others in the name of Christ as that may be necessary. In either case these persons leave behind the conning and controlling, the manipulating endemic to the rescuer/martyr roles, and enable persons to engage in authentic rescues and real martyrdom as God may lead.

In the process "messiahs" are replaced with loving disciples of The Messiah. Partners have no illusion that they can or must meet the needs of the entire world, carrying the sin and suffering of the world on their shoulders. They make the discipleship-recovery journey as followers of Messiah Jesus. They understand the implications of affirming that through Him, not through themselves, God has worked reconciliation of all persons to himself (Eph. 2:14 ff.). They learn not to confuse their participation in that peace (2:14–22; 4:1–6) with the establishing of it for all human beings.

Miracle: Partners from Erstwhile Parasites

The character transformation set before us in this journey represents nothing short of a miracle. Paul envisions that erstwhile thieves (v. 28) will by the grace of God wind up as partners, reaching out to meet the needs of others around them with integrity. In contrast to their parasitic past, they will not be setting up needy ones for an emotional or financial or spiritual or sexual hit of some sort, or otherwise be conning them. They will not be meeting their needs primarily as a way of meeting their own needs. They will, miracle of miracles, actually be sharing with those in need out of their own strength. And in the process they will fulfill their destiny and mirror the authentic, giving love of their Father. This is the journey *From Parasite to Partner*.

Questions for Reflection

1. How much time and energy do I devote to persons from whom I do not want something?

2. How much do I expect other people to "cover for me" and do maintenance tasks necessary to community life—turn off lights, clean up floors, put away clothes, do dirty dishes, put away tools, take hair out of the shower, etc.?

3. Would our family survive if everyone spent money at the rate I expect to?

4. Do I confuse wholehearted surrender to God with the destruction of myself? Am I afraid to ask for what I want or to take care of my own needs for fear of being selfish?

5. Do I actually allow myself to embezzle funds, shoplift, or otherwise steal, and wind up thinking it's somehow OK?

6. Am I willing to be part of a group of authentic persons that risk sharing their actual needs as well as their victories?

7. Am I prepared to take responsibility for my own actions and resources as an act of trust in God?

8. If everyone spoke as I do, or refrained from speaking, would the groups I live in be able to function well or even survive?

9. Have I expected persons of the opposite sex or institutional watchdogs to take responsibility for monitoring my sexual behavior to prevent me from abusing or violating others' sexual boundaries?

10. Can I trust God to do for me what I have never been able to do for myself, face my parasitic ways, and take responsibility for myself?

From Toxic Talk to Constructive Communication

(Ephesians 4:29–30)

The Way "The Thompson Men" Talk to "Their Women"

As we drove home from a visit to Minnesota not many years into our marriage, Ede opened her heart in a rare moment of candor. "When we visit the Thompson relatives in Minnesota," she confided, "you begin to talk to me just like the Thompson men talk to their women." Say what?! I wasn't aware "the Thompson men" *had* a way they talked to "their women." The very idea!

She explained. They talked down to women, insulted them, demeaned them. I didn't normally talk this way to her, she hedged. But at home in Minnesota I tended to talk to her in these ways, she said, and she felt hurt by that.

We agreed that such ways of treating anyone, especially a spouse, were certainly not pleasing to God and not what we wanted in our marriage. We would work together to be aware of how we were communicating. It did not occur to either of us to ask *why* I found myself treating her in these ways.

Unfortunately, as our agendas of contention lingered unresolved, I replicated more and more those "Thompson men" patterns with which I had been raised. Just as unfortunate perhaps, that candor on Ede's part was not often repeated over the next twenty-plus years. Both of us increasingly engaged in a variety of communication patterns fraught with problems. Sad to say, Gina would one day confront me with the fear and helplessness she had experienced as a child—helplessness to protect her mother from my tongue! This child's fears were only one of the consequences of the multifaceted toxic talk common in our family. No wonder Paul takes up speech patterns as part of the discipleship-recovery journey.

The Teaching

Stop letting rotten talk come from your mouth,
but speak whatever is good for building up another as you
  see their need,
in order that your speech may give grace to those who hear.
And [in this matter of your speech as elsewhere]
stop grieving God's Holy Spirit,
by whom you have been marked as God's person
until the day of redemption (AOT).

Here Paul takes up the most obvious barometer of personal and family health. Patterns of communication provide the conduit through which the various features of a person's or family's health or dysfunction move. They express what is really in a family. For this reason, this aspect of the discipleship-recovery journey might well stand near the front of the list in helping persons diagnose their own and their family's soundness. Virginia Satir ranks communication as "the largest single factor" determining what kinds of relationships a person establishes with his world.[1]

This page in the road map of the journey follows the same contours as those before. The first leg calls for bringing toxic communication to a halt, and assumes the identification of this behavior as a prerequisite to stopping it. The second leg turns to the adoption of patterns of communication that actualize our destiny of holy love. Speech can be *toxic;* it can also be *tonic.* So through their communication, individual disciples join the Christian community and its ministers (4:12, 16) in "building up" others.

Then, as with the journey to disclosure (v. 25) and to partnership (v. 28), the motivation cited here (v. 29) assumes a radical reorientation in holy love. The apostle envisions persons dispensing grace, not poison, with their words.

We take the exhortation in verse 30 about grieving the Holy Spirit as intended to stand in tandem with the teaching about communication. The dynamic equivalent translation, *"And in this matter of your speech as elsewhere,"* makes this explicit. As a general exhortation in a series of otherwise specific teachings, one expects it not to stand alone but to be linked with the immediately preceding context, as is the warning regarding the Devil in verse 27 with which it seems to stand in parallel. This tandem teaching shows the keen interest of God's Spirit in this agenda. And it emphasizes the importance of the issue at stake. By its warning it also brings to the fore the letter's encouragement regarding the power of God's Spirit to effect the transformation envisioned in this aspect of the discipleship-recovery journey.

Stop Toxic Talk

The Lethal Power of Speech

The translation "rotten speech" echoes closely the apostle's word choice.[2] "Rotten" brings to the topic of speech the same noxious connotations it had with rotten fish (Matt. 13:48).

Paul's word choice may well have sprung from more than stylistic considerations for picturesque language, for Scripture from page one reveals the tremendous power of the spoken word. Genesis, chapter 1, shows the cosmos-generating power of God's creative word. Here Paul pictures the tremendously destructive power of unloving speech. We know it's lethal.

Obviously Destructive Speech

The destructive nature of some forms of speech are widely recognized. We know abusive, violent, vulgar, degrading talk hurts people. We may not realize *how* profoundly and deeply it destroys persons. The physical, sexual, emotional, intellectual, and spiritual abuse that generates core shame almost always carries a verbal abuse component.[3] Screaming, name calling, threatening, and ridiculing constitute emotional abuse, even when they are aimed at someone else and we are forced to listen.[4] When children grow up experiencing these assaults on themselves or others dear to them, they are injured. Unconscionable numbers of homes, ruled by fear and intimidation thick enough to cut, have this abuse for their standard fare. An unfortunate number of "good" families experience outbursts of this abuse, seriously affecting the family members and undermining efforts to transmit faith and health. Wed with other forms of physical or sexual abuse, the damage just compounds.

Speech and Communication

The nature of communication explains this lethal impact at least in part. This is because we deal not simply with words but with the whole cluster of components that make up the communication event. Words do not travel by themselves, but in the company of a whole complex set of signals sent with them. Words come packaged with body language, emotional signals, tone of voice, and assumed thoughts. All of these, such as body language, are incredibly complex and variegated. Thus, threatening words rarely come as a clinically delivered message. With the threatening words travel threatening gestures that intimidate and portend violence, facial expressions that say "I am angry" or "I hate you" or "I'm going to kill you." Tense muscles and exaggerated breathing add their point. Voice tone says "I'm dead serious about this" or, "I'm about to go over the edge here" or, "If I weren't such a good Christian, I'd maim you." And so it goes.

As we shall see, this complexity of communication only increases when the verbal message does not match the other components. This explains why 140–decibel rock music about love or an evangelist's "harangue voice" message about God's love are equally dysfunctional and litter the communication process with contradictory messages. Threats delivered in a "loving" or "clinical" voice may prove even more damaging than those sent with more congruent body-voice data.

So, when Paul talks about toxic talk and words that give grace, he is actually broaching the whole question of verbal communication and the complex set of subcommunications that comprise it. "Stop letting rotten talk come out of your mouth" surely begins with facing and repudiating those obvious forms of abusive speech that destroy people. It begins by facing squarely all rationalizations which minimize these assaults on others—"I flew off the handle;" "My family all talked like this;" "The kids know I don't mean it." It means coming to terms with the shame that drives such behavior, learning new ways of relating, and choosing those ways by the grace of God.

Tolerated Speech Toxins: Communication Blocks

In many families the damage occurs not with obviously abusive outrage, but with equally toxic forms of speech usually tolerated, if not actually applauded by our culture. These patterns of communication are now recognized even in business and professional life as "counterproductive," because they "block communication." Here are some of the most common.[5]

Command Mode. Barking commands like a marine sergeant blocks normal communication. "Get supper for us!" "Shut up!" "Pick up your room!" "Get to work!" These may "get the job done" for a while, but in the end, real communication grinds to a halt.

Here, as with several of these "communication blocks," we recognize that in specific, peculiar situations a command is exactly what is called for. A child about to step into the path of a truck needs to hear *and* obey a command; there may not be time for reasons. But we cannot appeal to these special cases to justify a mode of relating to our spouse or children or employees or associates regularly in the "command mode."

Placating-Distracting. "There now, that wasn't so bad, was it?" "When I had that surgery, I was in the hospital twice as long as you've been." "Here, have a cookie. Take a drink." "It was just a pet." Placating or distracting says that what you claim is important is not important. It says that what you think hurts doesn't really hurt that bad. It denies your intelligence and ability to assess what you think and feel. A lifetime of placating/distracting does serious damage to self-esteem.

Psychologizing. Unless one has been asked for psychological insight, or the conversation is about such issues, attempts to explain another's actions by offering psychological analysis block communication. "You did that, because you're so insecure." "You're feeling guilty about things that don't matter." "You're acting out your mother's garbage." Psychologizing claims to know motives hidden from the persons themselves. Such psychologizing often fails to deal with people as they are, and sends the message that you know people better than they know themselves.

Interrogating. There are times when one should and must ask for information. But interrogating persons like a detective probing for evidence is an assault that blocks communication. "Where were you last night?" "How fast were you going?" "Why didn't you call me?" "How much did you get paid?" "What did you do with your money?" Interrogation conveys the message that you suspect others of something, or that you do not trust them or respect their judgment.

Moralizing and Advice-Giving. Telling others what they should do, must do, ought to do is moralizing. "You should get up earlier." "The right and just thing for you to do is . . ." "A person who claims the sort of religion you have should . . ." "God's will here means . . ." Of course, there are times when we are called upon to render moral judgments on behavior and possible courses of actions. Not all behaviors are equally acceptable, and some are downright evil. But relating to others habitually in the moralizing or advice-giving mode tells them you know better than they what is right and wrong. Our family called this habit of mine "pontificating."

Sarcasm. This stock-in-trade of the Thompson family's male members blocks communication by sending double and contradictory messages. "Well, that was really smart, wasn't it?" when you mean, "That was not wise at all." "What a feast!" when you mean, "What a pitiful excuse for a meal!" With its mixed messages, sarcasm confuses. It forces family members and associates to try to figure out what one really means—a waste of valuable mental energy. Sarcasm assaults, because it almost always masks anger. Persons who live with these attacks suffer a considerable toll over time. I will not soon forget my shock when Gina finally shared her fear for her mother in the face of my relentless sarcasm. I had never seen it that way.

Lecturing or "Know-It-Alling." Lecturing or "know-it-alling" tells others you think you know more than they do about almost anything under discussion. It calls their attention to information or resources that any thinking persons obviously should have thought of before venturing to do or say what they did. It calls into questions their own ability to think and bring information to bear. Often persons want and need many other things—e.g., sympathy, careful listening, affirmation of authentic interest—before they need information. As a dominant mode of relating to others it blocks communication.

Indirection. "Indirection" does not speak directly what the speaker thinks, feels, needs, or wants. "Wouldn't you like to sit by the window?" when you mean, "I want you to sit by the window." "Who'd like to go to church tonight?" when you mean, "I want to go to church tonight, and I'd like you to go with me." Indirection blocks communication not only by failing to give adequate information, but also by attempting to manipulate others. More seriously, it often comes accompanied by guilt dumping. Now the hearers not only do not know what you want, but they feel guilty when they don't respond appropriately—a double-barreled attack on self-worth.

Critiquing. Though there are times when one's job or the situation calls for honest, forthright critique, the "critique mode" as regular fare in any relationship blocks communication. The critiquer finds the *C* on a report card first before he comments on the two *B*s and three *A*s that are also there. The critiquer finds flaws, locates mistakes, sees errors, points out bloopers, spots inadequacies, highlights failures, and in general fixes on what is *not* OK in everything—you name it. The critique may come with sarcasm or with great kindness and alleged concern. It may even come after lots of positive preparation. But it will come. The message is: "You, your behavior, ideas, accomplishments, opinions, products, property, and person are not good enough for me. Sorry. I'm superior." This mode unhappily undermined my own ability to relate positively to my wife and children.

Computing. Analytical gifts and clear thought are rare treasures in our confused world. But "computing" brings a solely analytical approach to all conversations and topics. Like a scientist or an engineer at work on an intractable problem, the computer analyzes, categorizes, computes, and figures all the angles, and reads out a solution. Depreciating emotional factors as soft-headed, it insists on approaching all problems with unsullied rationality. It evades by reducing life to solely cognitive functions and winds up demeaning others who wish to insist on a larger spectrum for human communication.

Mind Reading. Mind reading claims to know what another person is thinking and feeling, an impossible claim. "You want me to feel bad, that's why you do this." "You like to be controlled, I know." Mind readers finish sentences for spouses, children, and friends. They speak for other persons without authorization. Mind readers attempt to control outcomes and to manipulate while sending the message that others cannot think or speak for themselves. They "know better."

Core Shame Delivery System

The reason these speech patterns actually "block communication" is because in one way or another they all demean or assault other human beings. Along with the more obviously abusive speech noted before, they constitute most of the delivery system in the self-perpetuating cycle uncovered in the creation database. These patterns of communication deliver the shame of shame-based people.

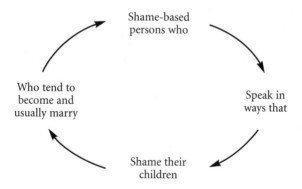

These patterns of communication solidify the family system, forming part of the trap and generating increasing problems.

Because these speech habits are so common, we are prone to dismiss them as the harmless creations of well-meaning but overzealous counselors. But this will not do. These speech habits constitute an integral part of the web of delusion and distortion that permeates dysfunctional families.[6] They are part of the coping strategies developed by hurting children and carried to their detriment into adult life. Their seriousness can scarcely be exaggerated. "If you want to make your body sick, become disconnected from other people, throw away your beautiful brain power, make yourself deaf, dumb, and blind, using the four crippling ways of communication [she names placating, blaming, computing, and distracting] will in great measure help you to do it," Satir says.[7]

Jesus taught that as the fruit of the tree reveals its character, so the words of a person reveal the heart. "Out of the abundance of the heart the mouth speaks," He said. Regarding this He continued, "The good person from his [or her] good treasure brings out good things; the bad person from bad inner treasure brings out bad things" (Matt. 12:34–35 AOT). Stopping toxic talk, then, means not only identifying toxic talk but facing the "heart," our real selves. The program Paul points us to carries us forward on that journey.

Cultivate Constructive Speech

"But," Paul says to these believers at Ephesus, "in contrast to the rotten talk now found in your communication, speak whatever is good for building up another as you see their need" (v. 29). Learning what it means to live in holy love involves learning to speak not only in ways that do not harm but also in ways that actually build up. Thus, acquiring communication skills to carry out this vision constitutes a powerful part of the discipleship-recovery journey.

Learning to "Level"

Over against the four main destructive communication patterns she has seen in thirty years of working with people, Satir puts what she calls "leveling." Leveling describes as well as any word I know the constructive speech the disciple is after. In leveling,

> All parts of the message are going in the same direction—the voice says words that match the facial expression, the body position, and the voice tone. Relationships are easy, free, and honest, and there are few threats to self-esteem. With this response there is no need to blame, retreat into a computer, or to be in perpetual motion. Of the five responses [Satir considers] only the leveling one has any chance to heal ruptures, break impasses, or build bridges between people.[8]

At the least, leveling involves speaking "your own reality."[9] Speaking your own reality means speaking reality as you perceive it. This may seem trite, of course, since one may think we really have no other choice. We can speak only what we perceive. But the process attracts problems at two points: 1) adequacy in perception and, 2) capacity to speak. Unfortunately, the perception adult children have of their own reality and that of others is badly skewed, making this "simple" endeavor an ordeal at times. But their skewed perception of reality poses only half the problem. Their difficulty speaking it constitutes the other half. They have become so accustomed to thinking and speaking about their reality as others want them to, that in some cases they have nearly lost the capacity to speak their own reality. They spend their lives actually speaking other people's reality.

- Constructive speech speaks about one's own body.[10] Disciples do this when they actually see their own appearance accurately and are aware of how their bodies are functioning, *and* have gained the freedom to speak for themselves.

- Constructive speech speaks about one's own thinking. We do this when we know what our thoughts really are and gain confidence and freedom to put those thoughts clearly into words.

- Constructive speech speaks about one's own feelings. Disciples do this when they become aware that they have feelings without being overwhelmed by them and learn to put those feelings into words.

- Constructive speech speaks about one's own behavior. Disciples take this ground when they become aware of what they actually are doing, acknowledge that behavior and speak candidly and clearly about it.

Speaking "our own reality" may sound self-centered at first hearing. But a moment's reflection shows that these freedoms open us to the entire range of speaking needed to actualize our destiny of holy love. For instance, speaking my own thinking calls me to take clear ownership for my views about God, others, and self, about health and illness, about every question from cosmology and theodicy to pediatrics and parenting. Speaking my feelings allows me to share with others in clear words my compassion for them, my longings, and my aspirations. In other words, speaking my own reality means not focusing solely on myself, but having the capacity and freedom to speak authentically and redemptively.

Listening for Another's Needs

Paul calls attention to the constructive speaker's focus on "the need," the need of another and the need at hand. Thus constructive communication involves not simply speaking but attentive listening as well. Constructive speech is not "one-way eloquence," but participation in a full-spectrum communication. As do others, Bradshaw and Satir emphasize *active listening* as an indispensable part of the communication process. Without it, communication does not occur—just talk. As Bradshaw explains, this is "listening for congruence, . . . a match-up between content and process, i.e., does their body match their words?" Active listening means "real contact" with others.[11]

For disciples "active listening" means genuine interest in another and careful attention to who they actually are, what they actually are doing, what they want and need. It involves growth in the ability to get out of myself enough to care about someone else. On the other hand, it may also mean growth in the capacity to distance myself enough from others as to be able to actually see *them* instead of my own needs projected or mirrored in them. And it means particular attention to need, for one is headed toward giving grace.

Giving Grace by Words

Giving grace to others provides the disciple's motive. One could speak constructively with attention to need for strictly pragmatic reasons—good business, less hassle, better "vibes," fewer ulcers. But Paul aims much higher than pragmatics (though this "pragmatic" reality is itself grounded in creation). The discipleship-recovery journey is heading toward incarnating the mind of Messiah here and now, and thus achieving our created destiny of holy love. Paul's "radical reorientation" in holy love surfaces again.

This unveils a marvelous discovery: human beings, like God Himself, can "give grace" through their words. They can "speak grace" to those around them, as did the Master. In this, as in the other features of the discipleship-recovery journey, they are invited to live "the truth as it is in Jesus" (4:21) and to "be imitators of God" (5:1). We reflect God's own creative speech power.

For instance, we can literally speak awareness of the good news of Jesus into existence for persons. Our culture's great confusion over Christian faith and biblical values, along with the church's unenviable record in siding with abusive governments and economies, has made authentic understanding and real hearing of the good news of Jesus an exceedingly rare event. The sort of communication Paul assumes greatly increases the possibility of actually speaking awareness of the "real" good news into existence for some associate.

We can *speak forgiveness* into being for some person in debt to us or another. We may even speak the forgiveness of God Himself to another in such a way that a face and voice is put on that forgiveness, enabling a needy one to appropriate it at last. Disciples of Jesus can speak *freedom to think and feel* into being for persons around us, at home, at church, in the office. Our words can grant persons freedoms they have never experienced in homes dominated by shame and emptied of meaningful freedom. We can speak into being the *liberty to act one's age,* creating the opportunity for them to be who God purposed them to be where they now are. These suggestions barely begin the ways in which we are empowered by God's Spirit to speak grace to others. What a marvel!

Claim God's Grace to Save You Here—Too

Some will already be thinking the likelihood of changing their speech patterns is about as great as their chance of changing the tide. The famous intractability of "the tongue" may illustrate for us as well as any of the agendas faced here the complex and terribly addictive nature of sin.

Complex, Addictive Nature of Sin

Few if any of the addictive-compulsive, codependent behaviors of adult children (or "normal" people) are simple matters of one clear choice. This is certainly true of the behaviors encountered in the discipleship-recovery journey projected by Paul.

Sin is complex in at least two ways: 1) in the number of choices involved in sin, and 2) in the nature of the choices involved. Regarding the "number" of choices involved in "a sin," there comes a time, of course, when we choose to speak words. But that choice of utterance does not stand isolated from the complex set of choices that have preceded and led to it. Some of these choices are ours— ways we have come to cope with core shame, interpretations we have come to accept of data coming from our environment. Some of the choices belong to other persons, like our primary caregivers. When and how I began to choose sarcasm, critiquing, and computing as my major modes of communicating I am not entirely sure. But it was not a matter of single, simple choice.

This leads to the second matter of complexity in sin, the nature of the choices involved. Some choices are made openly and knowingly. We know that vulgarity and blasphemy are beneath the love of a disciple of Jesus. But we may choose this mode of speech anyway, often acknowledging in the very process our awareness of wrong. Other choices we make in the sorts of sins addressed in the discipleship-recovery journey by the apostle are either not so clearly deliberate or are actually unintentional acts, *"unintentional sins,"* as

Scripture calls them. They are often sins of the sort treated most extensively and profoundly in Leviticus, chapters 4 and 5.

When we think of these Levitical situations of unintentional sin, we may think mainly of things like "touching any unclean thing" by mistake (Lev. 5:2 ff.) or similar "mechanical" or technical infractions of a long gone code. But the Torah's presentation has much more sophistication than that. The section on unintentional sin includes, for example, rash speech. "When any of you utter aloud a rash oath for a bad or a good purpose . . . and are unaware of it [unaware of uttering an oath?], when you come to know it, you shall in any of these be guilty" (Lev. 5:4).

Leviticus 5:15 raises the possibility of inadvertently committing "a breach of faith," as the RSV translates it. An "inadvertent" breach of faith? What is the meaning of such a thing? We are accustomed to seeing the Hebrew word *ma'al*—here translated "breach of faith"—carry the notion of "treachery" or "unfaithfulness" elsewhere in the Old Testament (as in Lev. 6:2). These seem anything but inadvertent or unknown (e.g., Lev. 26:40; Num. 5:6, 12, etc.; cf. similar breaches in 6:1–7).

It is possible that *ma'al* carries a specialized meaning here, peculiar to the worship setting. But it is equally possible, indeed I think more probable, that the word carries its normal meaning and that Torah intends to show the complexity of choice in human sin. Inadvertent sin addresses the matter of accountability, of responsibility. One becomes responsible, accountable, when the sin becomes known to the offender (Lev. 4:14, 23, 28 etc.). The breadth of behaviors included implies there are even behaviors one would think could never be "inadvertent" that may at times be just that. So it is with human sin.

And so it is with speech patterns and the other challenges in the discipleship-recovery journey mapped by Paul. Just what our awareness is in some of these choosings may be very difficult to determine. Someone else looking on may wonder how such behavior could possibly be "unintentional." And we cannot use this rubric as a screen to hide sin of which we are fully aware. Nevertheless, the complexity of choice encountered in these sins explains in good measure how we can aim so high and hit so low. How could we intend so well and do so poorly? Our family's communication patterns, my communication patterns, illustrate these tragedies so unfortunately well.

These "unintentional sins" are still sin (even before they come to one's awareness). They still need atonement, still call for change and for restitution where possible. The sinner here stands accountable. God calls these behaviors sin because of His interest in protecting His creatures and His own sense of holiness. They are sin, because they destroy persons and affront God, quite apart from what the doer intended.

Not only is sin complex, it is also addictive. As we have seen, the speech patterns exposed as abusive and toxic talk are themselves coping mechanisms of the addictive, compulsive, codependent person. These speech patterns are the conduits through which the various addictive and compulsive relationships travel. Without these there are no relationships. Breaking these habits, changing these patterns means altering ways of coping as deeply ingrained and tightly treasured as the alcoholic's alcohol. Some of them even carry their own highs of adrenaline. That is why the first step is "We admitted that we were powerless . . . that our lives had become unmanageable."

Walking in the Transforming Spirit

Powerless, but not without power. Here as at every turn of the discipleship-recovery journey this paradox meets us: We cannot change by ourselves; we cannot change without ourselves. The admonitions in these instructions are all addressed to us, to the readers: "*You* stop letting rotten talk come out of your mouths; *you* speak whatever is good for building up another as you see their need" (AOT). And yet, we have already been told that we are saved "by grace through faith," and that we are transformed by "the power at work within you" (Eph. 2:8; 3:20).

Paul puts the paradox before us once more in his talk of the Holy Spirit in chapter 4, verse 30:

And [in this matter of your speech as elsewhere]
stop grieving God's Holy Spirit,
by whom you have been marked as God's person
until the day of redemption (AOT).

He speaks negatively yet implies good news as well. The warning reminds disciples that God's Spirit has particular interest in the utterances of His people, though He retains interest in all our doings. By the Spirit Jesus carried on His ministry of proclaiming the good news of the Kingdom (Mark 1:9–15; 3:20–30). By this same Spirit persons utter wisdom, prophecy, and all kinds of edifying utterance in the church (1 Cor. 12–14). Therefore, the Spirit is particularly grieved when disciples speak in ways that poison the fellowship and destroy one another.

Paul further reminds these readers that this Spirit is the very Spirit whose presence marks them as God's people in this world. The "official mark" or seal identifying these persons as "God's person" is the Spirit Himself, producing the character of God in these believers in such measure that their identity as God's people is clear. Therefore, communication modes that undercut that identity are particularly unfortunate and bring grief to God and His Spirit.

We should not conjure pictures of God the Spirit sulking in a corner or dumping guilt on us like the martyrs we have confronted in our family. This "grief" names the authentic response of God, deeply committed to our redemption and passionately involved in the journey to bring us to our destiny of holy love. This is not the "unmoved mover" or the "without feeling God" of Greek philosophy, but the God and Father of Jesus. This is the God who is "touched with the feeling of our infirmities" (Heb. 4:15 KJV). Therefore the Spirit's grief itself carries promise for the journey.

If we trust these parts of our life to Him, surely He can be at work within us to bring about change here as elsewhere.

Questions for Reflection

1. Do I speak my mind and heart much at all, or do I expect my spouse or children or friends to read my mind?
2. Is my speech really a medley of communication blocks?
3. Do I trivialize my sarcasm as "just me," or "a bad habit," when in reality it is poison?
4. Do I order persons around, telling them what to do, think, and feel?

5. Do I talk "just like Dad/Mom" in spite of the fact that I swore I would never repeat their ways?

6. Have I ever thought seriously about the speech habits of the home I grew up in?

7. Do I hide behind the fact that "I don't mean to hurt people" as a way of avoiding responsibility for my toxic talk—when God calls it sin?

8. Do I grieve God's Spirit by acting as though my toxic talk is beyond the reach of God's grace and the power of His Spirit?

9. Have I given up hope of ever changing my well-worn speech paths?

10. If God opens the way of holy love to me in my talk, can't He surely, won't He surely help me if I admit my need, throw myself on His grace, and appropriate the resources for change He is putting in my hands?

From Rage
to Reconciliation
(Ephesians 4:31–32)

From Baseball to Battering

The play was a close one, the call a disaster. Rob and Ed had been watching the season opener with their families as they'd done for years, this year at Rob and Angie's place. The men each saw the play differently, as they frequently did. But this time their "debate" over the call had gone no more than a few exchanges when it took on a life of its own and spiraled out of control.

Ed launched into a tirade, shouting, berating, and threatening Rob, while their petrified wives stood speechless. Ed began throwing articles around, then curiously started opening and closing the front door, jerking it open and slamming it shut, practically jarring it from its hinges. The knob actually dislodged. He kicked in the bottom window of the storm door and, as a parting shot, bashed in the top sash as well! All this damage to an old friend's home over a bad call by an umpire!

Later that weekend Ed came back to apologize to Rob. He was terribly sorry for what had happened, and really didn't try to explain the explosion. He would pay for the damage, of course. But when Rob and Angie came to talk about how they should or could go about rebuilding their relationship with Ed, it was clear this violent outburst of rage had jarred them to the core. Apologies and repayment notwithstanding, the terms of their friendship had been altered.

Upon reflection they realized that, although Ed had never lost control of himself in this fashion in their presence before, his role as an intimidating, verbally abusive "friend" was not really new. Rob had to admit that he had absorbed a good bit of attack over the years in perpetuating something of a Laurel and Hardy, odd-couple friendship—funny, perhaps, but more painful than humorous, now that he thought about it. Beyond that, Rob knew Ed's temper was infamous in his family; he was euphemistically known as a very "intense" man.

The Thompson family's dysfunctions happened not to include rage of this sort. But stories like Rob and Ed's prove commonplace in our hurting world. They provide the scripts in which women and children are battered and physically and emotionally abused, even maimed and killed—all too often in Christian families.

Rage. It's no fiction of the apostle's imagination. And it's not confined to barroom brawls. Ephesians 4:31–32 peels the scab off a messy sore in human relationships and offers healing by the grace of God.

The Teaching

Let all bitterness and rage and shouting and abusive speech be removed from you along with every sort of bad feeling.[1] *Become kind to one another, tenderhearted, forgiving one another, just as God in Messiah forgave you (AOT).*

Paul returns to his second topic of anger again, but with a different issue in mind this time. Verses 26–27 addressed carrying and nursing anger. Here loud, violent, out-of-control anger seems to be the negative point; hence the translation "rage." Behind this point stands a larger agenda raised by the apostle's word choices and his positive instruction in verse 32. The vocabulary of verse 31 carries heavy feeling freight: bitterness, passionate anger, malice.

"Passionate anger" might translate the two words, used together for emphasis, which I have rendered "rage." The one denotes angry outbursts of rage (cf. Rev. 12:2), the other anger lingering. The last word, translated "malice" by the NRSV and others, "takes in any attitude or action which intends harm to one's neighbor."[2] But the New English Bible has caught the verse's emphasis correctly, in my judgment, by translating "bad feeling of every kind," and thereby focusing this word's wide meaning on the attitudinal side indicated by its context here.

This hunch regarding the feeling freight of verse 31 is confirmed by a key word in verse 32 translated "tenderhearted." The word reflects awareness ancient and modern that intense feeling registers in the viscera, the belly. So, much as we talk of "gut feelings," this word and a related verb attach a prefix meaning "good" to the word for "viscera" (remember the KJV, "bowels and mercies," Phil. 2:1) and carries the meaning of "compassionate" or "tenderhearted." It is an expression of intense feeling and again sets the tone for the surrounding vocabulary which already addresses attitudes of kindness and forgiveness. So these exhortations call persons on the discipleship-recovery journey to be done with the feelings and voice and words of rage. They invite us to become tender persons, feeling and acting as God did when He forgave us in Messiah.

This comparison of the disciple's attitude to that of God Himself in Messiah takes the motivation for the journey in a slightly different direction than we have seen to this point. The radical "love reorientation" that leads the disciple from self-preoccupied, destructive relationships to authentic interest in the needs and well-being of others is here replaced by the motive to embody in our journey the heart of God Himself. The behavior and attitudes of the Creator become both the pattern guiding us and the magnet drawing us on. The concluding instruction will reason similarly (5:2).

Distance Yourself from the Rampage

A Single, Ugly Picture: Rage

Verse 31 in the Greek text names six different evils: bitterness, wrath, anger, wrangling, slander, malice (following the NRSV). But these look more like closely painted, overlapping, dark hues of a single ugly picture than they do six, separate colors on a palate or clearly distinct blocks on a mosaic. They paint the picture of anger on the loose. This anger shouts, screams, spews bitterness, ridicule, and abuse on bystanders. This picture has fists clenched, fingers pointed, teeth showing, eyes blazing, heart pounding, and venom spilling everywhere. Although the apostle does not go beyond words in his list, pictures of child and spouse abuse will always include the colors from this collage. This is "rage."

Rage as a Response to Abandonment

Rampage can be a whole way of life. The fact that this rage presents a response totally out of proportion to the stimuli prompting it provides a clue that much more is going on than simple response to present woes. Rage waves a red flag. It announces a huge "being wound," core shame, as Bradshaw described it.

Common in alcoholic and other dysfunctional families, rage is itself an addiction. It "serves a self-protective function by insulating the self against exposure and by actively keeping others away."[3] Beyond this, as Paul's words have implied, rage is a whole body experience, releasing toxins into the system and addicting one to adrenaline highs as well. In other words, rage is another of the defenses adult children use to salve their pain and "solve" their problem. Not only does rage function as the other addictions do, but persons who rage (and their victims) experience the same cycle of shame, remorse, promise to reform, and relapse that other addicts experience. "Rage-aholic" is no joke.

Rage, better than the other addictions, actually puts a face on the intense anger associated with core shame, and is itself a powerful shame transfer agent.[4] Describing the feelings of women raised in alcoholic homes, Wilson finds "anger . . . too pallid a label for the *deep, internal rage*" these women report (my emphasis).[5] Firestone, we recall, emphasized that core shame involves this anger turned in on oneself. He expressed amazement at the astounding degree of "volatile emotions of murderous rage and self-hatred" expressed by many of his patients, self-hate with a "passion and intensity" far surpassing "anything they consciously thought they felt toward themselves."[6] Rage is this high-voltage anger on the loose. As Bradshaw explains, "Since the anger [experienced by abandoned children] is strictly forbidden, it is either projected onto others, turned against self or 'acted out,' or processed in complex combinations of these strategies."[7]

"Ragers" often are children of physical and sexual abuse. One may think first here of "angry young men." This is not surprising, because little boys more often than girls "identify with the violent offender and become offenders."[8] But rage poses a problem not just for males but for females as well, as we saw in Wilson's remark about the "deep, internal rage" of female adult children of alcoholics. Among biological parents, Bradshaw actually reports mothers involved as offenders in physical abuse slightly more than fathers.[9]

Repeatedly we return to our use of the "alcoholic" family or "adult children of alcoholics" as sadly prototypical of all families and the traces of childhood trauma they leave on their adults. We have seen how these more troubled families and persons paint in starker strokes the troubles plaguing all families and persons. Their tragedy allows others to see themselves more clearly. No families we have discovered are perfect; no adults totally without pain. The issue of rage drives this tragedy of the human predicament home. Firestone's experience around this issue broke down the wall between therapists and patients in a surprising discovery:

> My associates and I came to the conclusion that everybody has a considerable amount of deep-seated pain and sadness that they are continually suppressing, and indeed, may be completely unaware of in their everyday lives. It seemed that no one was immune to this deep primal pain, that no one had escaped childhood without being scarred to some extent ... We found no fundamental difference in this regard between the patients seeking therapy and the professionals and friends who volunteered to go through this process. In other words, there are not two categories of people, those with pain and those without it—everyone in our sample population had repressed pain and everybody's life centered around the avoidance of it.[10]

"The rampage" puts one more face on the deep tragedy in human sin and alienation from God. It opens one more window on the need for all persons to make the discipleship-recovery journey.

Facing Abuse in Christian Homes

Wife battering and child abuse present such a sad tragedy in Christian homes that any talk of "rage" which fails to mention this matter would be suspect. We specifically target "*wife* battering" here, because the amount of serious injury to husbands at the hands of their wives is statistically insignificant compared to the more frequent and more serious damage done to women by the men who "love" them. And, compared to its response to child abuse, the church's reaction to this problem of battered women has been disappointingly lethargic. In their potent book, *Battered Into Submission: The Tragedy of Wife Abuse in the Christian Home*, James and Phyllis Alsdurf report studies indicating three to four million women are beaten annually by their husbands in this country and two thousand to four thousand women are beaten to *death* in this violence![11] Sadly, all too many of these women were partners in a Christian marriage.

Several matters particularly related to our *God's Healing for Hurting Families* agendas interest us here. First, rage at work in wife battering parades the complex delusion problems we saw earlier. "Craziness," confused thinking, thoroughly muddled rationalizations and interpretations on the part of all parties abound in homes where women are battered. Battering husbands will typically blame their wives for their own madness and/or will claim a right to this sort of "handling" of their "women." Frequently they refuse to acknowledge the sin and wrong involved. Sadly, battered wives for various reasons often accept this delusion and blame themselves for their husbands' violence. Complicating all of this are grotesque misunderstandings of the "submission" of wives mentioned in Scripture (as in Eph. 5:22 ff.) as warrant both for the tyranny and "submission" perpetrated.[12]

The church, especially the conservative church, has too long and too often been a partner in this delusion. Its legitimate commitment to marriage and against divorce has led it to encourage women to remain in abusive and threatening marriages, often to the neglect of other equally compelling biblical principles. And its unfortunate tendency to understand apostolic teaching about the submission of wives to husbands in terms of a hierarchy or a "chain of command" has time and again played directly into the hands of an outrageously abusive husband. Further, its ignorance about the actual dynamics of abuse and the complex set of reasons that lead women to stay in abusive relationships has more often than not found pastors and Christian counselors laying *on the battered wife* both the majority of the blame for the abuse and the major responsibility for bringing it to a halt!

Battering shows the same profiles of addictive behavior we have encountered elsewhere. Typically couples repeatedly exhibit three phases of the battering experience. In the first phase, the wife blames herself for her husband's explosions and accepts his self-serving justifications for the misery. In the second phase, the husband's accumulating rage and brooding often prove so frightening and overwhelming that the wife may actually trigger the confrontation to "be done with it." Finally, after the beating follows a time of mutual pleasantness, contrition, and placating, in which the abuser is obsessed with concern for his wife. The delusion: this final, uneasy calm gets cemented in place as the picture of "normal" life in the family. The battering gets minimized as exceptional, whereas in reality it controls the entire family's life.

Beyond these insanities, batterers are notorious manipulators, nearly "dual personalities." They show amazing skills at suave seduction to get what they want, but then startling rage and violence in response to finding themselves thwarted or denied. They and the entire family are sucked into perpetuating the lie that "Daddy" or "Reverend" or "Pastor" or "Brother So and So" is the kind, gentle Christian he seems to be at church and in public.[13]

As do other addicts, batterers perpetuate a family history of abuse and violence. Research shows roughly 60 percent of husbands who beat their wives were either beaten by their own fathers or saw their mothers beaten.[14] They carry into their marriages the profound insecurity and neediness of adult children, but cover it with their rage. As Paul Tournier put it, "Violence is a way of proving that one exists, when one believes oneself to be insignificant."[15]

The batterer gathers in a single, tragic person the whole set of needs addressed by the various teachings in Ephesians 4:25–5:2. A recent handbook aimed at helping men "live without violence" devotes chapters or sections to almost all of the issues we will have covered in our study.[16] Recognizing and resolving anger, expressing anger nonviolently, learning to listen, learning to communicate effectively, developing and respecting boundaries, and more occupy the man who wants to learn to live without violence.

Distancing from Rage

Whether the rage Paul describes actually leads to physical abuse or not, the rampage life he describes clearly has no place in the destiny of holy love to which God calls us. But how will the "distancing" be done?

Students working with various Bible translations will notice significantly different renderings of the exhortation verb in Ephesians 4:31. The RSV and NASB, for example, retain the passive voice[17] of the Greek text, with "Let all bitterness . . . *be put away* from you." NRSV, e.g., renders this passive of the Greek text with the "active voice:" "[You] *Put away* from you all bitterness . . ." The understanding reflected in the NRSV notes that all the other exhortations in this series are addressed actively to the readers— *the readers themselves* are to act. This interpretation considers the passive to be a stylistic variant here, not intended to indicate that *someone else*—God—is to do the putting away, the removing. This "putting away" would stand parallel to that in Ephesians 4:22.

The interpretation carried in the RSV and NASB, and in our translation, points to the fact that elsewhere the word used here does not appear in the passive without carrying passive meaning. I have stayed with this more traditional rendering for two reasons. First, I do not think the passive verb yields easily to being simply a stylistic variant for the active. Second, and perhaps more important for our discussion, the whole context of Ephesians (and biblical thought) will not allow an overly facile distinction between God's acting and the readers' acting in these issues of discipleship-recovery.

Of course God accomplished solely by Himself the historic acts of salvation on behalf of human beings—all the way from deliverance out of Egypt to redemption at the Cross. But in the features of the discipleship-recovery journey treated in 4:25–5:2 and elsewhere, the readers' choosing and God's enabling grace are inextricably joined. The translation brings to the fore the power of God to distance us from these destructive ways. The exposition intends to make clear that our learning, choosing, and relinquishing have much to do with releasing this power in our lives. From our side of the transactions, we can "repudiate the lie" about our rage and its many ramifications. We can commit to the journey of developing tenderness.

Develop Tenderness

Let Yourself Feel Again

All this talk of feelings may sound terrifically "wimpy," as Sandra Wilson warns in the opening lines of her chapter, "Released to Forgive Shame Givers," and very unrelated to Christian discipleship.[18] But believe it or not, learning to "be like Jesus" leads straight to learning to feel, among other things.

For many people this presents a major challenge, for the adult child's symptoms are all feeling-thinking disorders. Of the two— thinking and feeling—the feeling component often flows deeper, for it takes shape even in preverbal experiences.[19]

Our symptoms are unhealthy mechanisms that we use to keep from feeling our feelings. They smother, hide, distort and mix up our feelings. They turn fear and sadness into rage. They create depression from anger; fear from loneliness.[20]

In addition to the "distorting" and "mixing up" of feelings these persons feel, they and others experience "smothered" and "hidden" emotions. They have become numb from long, hard practice at denying their feelings. Energies normally invested in "feeling feelings" are invested instead in countering them. Bradshaw lists "tensing, internal talking, and shallow breathing" among the "counterenergies" mustered. "After years and years of practice, we can literally no longer feel our emotions."[21] These feeling skills were simply lost or never acquired in the developmental skips suffered by children in troubled families.

Wilson's concept of THOUGHT/feelings and thought/FEELINGS is helpful here, reminding us of Paul's link of thinking-feeling in his critique of the darkened mind (Eph. 4:17–18). It indicates that thoughts and feelings are never far or neatly separated, though one or the other may predominate in given considerations. "Cognitive restructuring" is critical, as we have seen in our reflection on the discipleship-recovery journey from delusion to disclosure. But Wilson warns her readers to remember that "when we are counseling for mind renewal with adult children of alcoholics, we are working for the restoration of feelings, which must be 'renewed' if profound growth is to occur."[22] In other words, as our family's sadness demonstrates, it proves easier to read and even write books about core shame, numbness, and recovery than it is actually to learn to be a human being with feelings again. Professorial types like me are particularly inclined to get bogged down in analysis of their problems and evaluation of various theories that explain them. We get seriously delayed in appropriating any approach and in pressing on through to get at our feelings which may defy analysis.

This absolute imperative of moving on past mind to heart explains why Wilson's strategies go beyond helping such persons explore their family's expressions of, messages about, and misbeliefs about feelings (i.e., cognitive restructuring). Persons in renewal must also learn to speak accurately of feelings, identify feelings, and express feelings appropriately—skills missed or skipped in childhood development in troubled families.[23]

This learning to identify, speak, and express feelings can transpire in private reflection, conversation with trusted friends, writing in a journal or prayer book, and in intentional living. For some this will mean acquiring virtually a new vocabulary to talk and think about areas of our lives largely ignored to this point—words like love, loathe, happy, sad, calm, anxious, peaceful, troubled, pleased, angry, affirmed, demeaned, healed, hurt, wakened, numbed, engaged, shut down, and on and on.

In *Released from Shame*, Sandra Wilson suggests other action strategies (adapted here) for learning to express one's feelings appropriately.[24]

- Make an inventory of the addictions you use to deaden your emotions, and
- Get help immediately to stop using these painkillers.
- Get help even if your addictions "appear" less deadly, like food (i.e. "'stuffing your feelings' by stuffing your face").
- Study a photo of yourself before age ten and allow yourself to remember how confused, scared, sad, lonely, or angry you felt. Ask the child what he or she needed in those distressing situations and, if possible, make arrangements to secure that support now: something to cuddle, a true friend who cares and listens, safe hugs, etc.
- Write about your fear of abandonment, reflecting the changed realities of your adult life, practicing new shame-free choices about handling your feelings.
- Practice less harmful ways of handling your anger than exploding. Try exercise, writing, painting, or drawing.
- Learn respectful assertiveness techniques so you don't need anger to shield you from personal boundary violations. For example, try the "broken record" approach (you continue to matter-of-factly state your desire or preference until the boundary-invading "other" realizes you are not backing down).

These provide places to start, at least, in charting new directions for learning to feel.

Develop Tenderness

Of course the discipleship-recovery journey in this case has much more in mind than simply or generally "learning to feel" (though perhaps we should caution once more against dismissing or trivializing this crucial learning). We are headed not just toward feeling. We are aiming at tenderhearted feelings and the redemptive relationships these can support with others.

Paul mentions two other features of tenderness here: kindness and forgiveness. These also involve learning for, as we have seen, many persons lack healthy notions of true "kindness" or "forgiveness." Learning the content of "tough love," love that protects the integrity and boundaries of others while acting in their behalf, would be a part of this journey. Learning the difference between authentic forgiveness and issuing "cheap grace" would be in the "lesson plans." Learning to "speak the truth in love" will be part of this development. Obviously then, much of the learning involved in the other strands of the journey covered will contribute to this development of tenderness.

Empathy. Empathy probably names the particular aspect of the journey pinpointed by the development of the tender heart, which is why we have spent so much time talking about feelings. Growing the tender heart takes us beyond not raging to the willingness to risk actually letting ourselves feel what someone else might feel. If we approach this from the viewpoint of developing intact boundaries, we set before us the vision of true intimacy. We set aside damaged or torn down walls on the one hand, or "shields up" defense on the other. We allow ourselves to enter the shoes of another person, to feel with them and for them in their joy or sadness, pain or gladness. Intact boundaries let us differentiate ourselves from others enough to enter their feelings without taking them all upon ourselves, without trying to fix their feelings or make them like ours.

If we come at this from the viewpoint of developing constructive communication, we remember Satir's and Bradshaw's instruction about active listening and whole-body communication. They stressed the truly significant challenge of actually hearing another person. Listening included being interested enough, attentive enough, free enough, and confident enough to actually open up to others. Empathy here means we learn to "listen" to the whole message being sent to us. We set aside preoccupation with what *we* are going to say, how we are going to answer, refute, deflect, or downplay what the other is saying and feeling. Instead we take it as a chief agenda in the discipleship-recovery journey to actually listen to another so as to be able to enter into their joy and pain. It is no accident that Paul includes this guide to empathy in his exposition of the "transformed mind:" "Rejoice with those who rejoice, weep with those who weep" (Rom. 12:15). This mind, he says, breaks the thought mold of pagan culture and is being truly renewed.

Return to the wife batterer for a moment. The Alsdurfs hold out cautious hope for this hard case rager. Among their "steps to reconciliation" they include, after confronting the evil, the *batterer's* feeling the pain. "Once the abuser has perceived that his wife's feelings about what he did are true, he begins to feel the pain he has inflicted on others. . . . And [this is]. . . something the batterer *should* feel. It is a sign of a repentant spirit."[25]

But empathy moves beyond individuals to groups, indeed to nations and races. Tenderheartedness for disciples of Jesus means this sort of listening, not just to persons in face-to-face conversation, but to other human beings in other cultures and places. It means listening across barriers that divide human beings, and reaching out to these persons with understanding and kindness.

These learnings foster tenderness, softness, gentleness. They engender the disposition to help, to support, to affirm, to discipline with understanding and kindness. They can even withstand evil with the desire to help and redeem.

Develop *Tenderness*

These learnings take time and constitute part of the journey. Commitment to them may take a moment. But the journey takes time. Paul may hint at this in his choice of words. Ephesians contains two "being" verbs common to the New Testament—one meaning simply "to be;" the other, which *can* designate more of a process, meaning "to be," "to become" or "to happen/occur." The two are often used interchangeably, so one dare not make too much of this distinction. Nevertheless, most of the uses of the second word in Ephesians make excellent sense with the more process-oriented meaning.[26] So the translation here calls for us to "become kind to one another, tenderhearted, forgiving one another." As we do this "becoming" we learn to emulate our Savior who has been "touched with the feeling of our infirmities" (Heb. 4:15, KJV). Indeed, according to the writer of the book of Hebrews, this very fact—that our high priest is by experience able "to sympathize with our weaknesses"—supports our commitment to stay true to the journey and to appeal to Him for help (Heb. 4:14–15, NRSV).

Remember How God Forgave You

Motivations for the Journey

As we have seen, Paul has appealed to several different motivations to support the discipleship-recovery journey. Verse 25 cited the reality of the human connection to build the journey from delusion to disclosure. Verse 28 raised the possibility of having something to share with persons in need as a motivating vision. Verse 29 inspired us with the possibility of actually giving grace through our words. All of these assumed an underlying reorientation in love, liberating adult children to be adult disciples, actualizing their destiny of holy love.

Here the apostle points to God Himself as our pattern for forgiveness and, by implication, for kindness and tenderheartedness as well. In Ephesians 5:2 he cites God's Messiah as the motivating example. He directs us from the vision of what we may become to the One who already embodies the holy love to which we are called. This example supports the journey in two ways. First, by providing instruction, the example shows us how we will forgive as we follow Him. Second, God's forgiveness, the fact of our forgiveness, and that of our fellow travelers provides the basis for our forgiving.

Costly (i.e., Authentic) Forgiveness

A sort of "pseudo-mutuality" pervades troubled homes and sets up disciples from such homes to issue what we have elsewhere called "cheap forgiveness."[27] (See the discussion in Chapter 5). The church's uneasiness with anger and other strong feelings, as well as sincere desires to foster peace and to follow Jesus can also lead to cheap forgiveness. As we saw in Chapter 5, cheap forgiveness is forgiveness that does not count the cost because it does not take the sin seriously enough.

At this point God's forgiveness in Christ provides a pattern for us, for God clearly takes our human sin very seriously. He regards sin as an assault on Himself and His creation, a breach of human destiny worthy of death and thoroughly alienating us from Him (Rom. 1:8–32). The enormity of our sin and our inability to do a thing about our moral debt to our Maker in part account for the costliness of His response, the giving of His Son (Rom. 3:20–28).

So, like God, in order to grant real forgiveness, we must stop minimizing wrong done to us by anyone, including our primary caregivers or present family and associates. We look their abuse and abandonment squarely in the face and still find grace to forgive.

Since we specifically opened the topic of wife battering earlier, we must caution clarity here. Forgiveness is possible and even desirable for these tragedies. But forgiveness does not mean tolerating abuse. And forgiveness does not necessarily mean continuing to live with an abusive husband. The Alsdurfs' wisdom at this point is pertinent. Because the batterer is a "master of false promises," in their "steps to reconciliation" they list the batterer's "promising to change" with this advice:

> Only a promise which comes after the batterer has faced his sin, felt his wife's pain and then confessed his sin, is a promise to be trusted . . . The authenticity of that promise will be tested through the fire of time and circumstances. The victim is right in waiting to see what fruit that promise will bear before reuniting with her husband, regardless of his impatience.[28]

Disciples do not confuse understanding *why* someone may have wronged us with the wrong itself. Understanding our parents' own heritage and families of origin may go a long way toward helping us understand why they behaved as they did. This does not alter the moral judgment one renders on abuse and abandonment, anymore than understanding the sources of our own pathologies excuses them or absolves us of responsibility for them.

Nor do we confuse estimating intention with forgiveness. Although some parents and "caregivers" are unworthy of the name and intend harm to their little ones, most parents and caregivers "do the best they can." They mean well. They love as they've been loved. As a matter of fact, the majority of darkness from which the discipleship-recovery journey leads us involves behavior of very complex and confused motivational origin, as we have seen. But what persons intend does not change the consequences of dysfunctional parenting and does not render abuse and abandonment benign. Persons who forgive authentically want to understand intentions as best they can, and these may figure in assessing the level of actual culpability involved. But in approaching forgiveness, disciples must look squarely at what happened to them—and still open their hearts for grace to forgive.

So, forgiving as God did in Christ involves costly forgiveness.

Empathetic Forgiveness

The emphasis in Ephesians on the seriousness of sin (2:1–3) and the "grace" by which we are saved implies this costliness, as does the description of Christ as an offering (5:2). But in view of the context, one wonders if the emphasis of God's forgiving example does not fall on the kindness, the tenderheartedness involved. The picture of salvation conveyed in "redemption" (1:7) implies this divine empathy. The word recalls the Old Testament image of God saving His people from bondage to the Egyptians (cf. Deut. 7:8; 9:26). Hearing their cry and their groaning and remembering His covenant, He saved them (Exod. 2:24–25). It evokes pictures of the Old Testament's "kinsman redeemer." Touched by his relative's desperate plight (who sold himself for unpaid debts), and moved to action, he pays his debt and secures his freedom (Lev. 25:48–49). Paul further describes God as demonstrating His lavish kindness in rescuing us from the power and penalty of sin (Eph. 2:7).

God's "in-Messiah" forgiveness models "empathetic forgiveness" par excellence. We call this event "Incarnation," because it involved God's coming "in human flesh," as 1 John 1:1–4 and 4:2 emphasize. As with the rest of the narrative of Messiah's life, Ephesians tells us almost nothing about this story—and other Pauline literature not much more. But, interestingly enough for our discussion, one of the few comments Paul makes about this "in human flesh" feature of the experience itself does focus exactly at the point of tenderness, compassion—the very sort of THOUGHT/feelings, thought/ FEELINGS featured in Ephesians 4:32. We alluded to the relevant word use (Phil. 2:1) in explaining the word "tenderhearted" in verse 31. In Philippians 2:1–11 Paul calls his readers to let the thinking-feeling mind of Messiah be in them. Thinking not of Himself but of others,

He emptied Himself to be born in human form. By implication this compassionate, tender mind would also be attributed to God.

The writer to the Hebrews explores this even more (4:14–16). Our high priest, Jesus, was tried as we are. Because of His experience of our situation He is "moved by the feeling of our infirmities." On this basis we appeal for help, knowing it makes a difference for God to have walked in our shoes.

So "forgiving one another as God in Christ forgave you" involves costly forgiveness. It also involves forgiveness that reaches out in tenderness, entering the shoes of another, and letting that person genuinely off the hook.

Wilson summarizes these insights well in "principles of forgiveness" she shares with persons seeking to be "released to forgive [even] the shamers." They are

- Principle 1: Forgiveness is a realistic view of the hurt and the hurters.
- Principle 2: Forgiveness is releasing the right to get even.
- Principle 3: Forgiveness requires admitting that forgiving is not merely difficult; it is humanly impossible.[29]

This is where the discipleship-recovery journey *From Rage to Reconciliation* leads.

Questions for Reflection

1. Do I "fly off the handle" or "lose my temper" a lot—in fact, really a lot, now that I think of it?

2. Have people in my family actually suffered bodily harm from my anger? Bruises? Black eyes? Scars or welts on their skin?

3. Have we had to tell the old "fell down the step" or "ran into the door" or "fell off the bike" stories to avoid exposing a family member's rage?

4. Have I ever connected my rampage to the anger experienced in my family of origin?

5. Have I ever tried to get in touch with the way I really feel about what I experienced as a child?

6. Do I dismiss talk of "feeling feelings" as "wimp talk" or mindless navel gazing? That is, do I trivialize a critical feature of human experience? Why?

7. Are kindness and tenderness among my discipleship agendas? In what way?

8. Have I thought of forgiveness mostly as a judicial, legal matter? What does God's tenderhearted forgiveness of me say about my own destiny as a disciple?

9. Do I expect people to tolerate my belligerence and loudness as "just me"?

10. If God can call me from darkness to light, can He not also help me with my terrible rage?

From Abandoned Waif to Well-Loved Child
(Ephesians 5:1–2)

Signs of Need

"You want to talk to *me*? You think what I had to say was worthwhile?" I could scarcely believe my ears.

I had just finished a series of presentations at a gathering of Free Methodist clergy from the northeast United States. "Doc, can we talk more about the questions you're covering this weekend?" Three or four former students of mine, then serving in local churches scattered across Pennsylvania and New York, gathered around me at the front of the auditorium. Animated, engaged, positive, they clearly liked what I had said. They thought it had considerable merit and relevance to their lives, and now wanted to pursue the discussion further.

I no longer recall the questions they raised or the issues we pursued. What I do recall most from that incident was a particular feeling: disbelief. I could scarcely assimilate the fact that these persons I respected actually valued me, my thinking, my ministry to them. For the first time I perceived how deeply and thoroughly I had come to discount myself. Realization of their apparently genuine regard for me, both personally and professionally, brought tears to my eyes. An intense sense of affirmation swept over me which I found hard to accept.

This strange encounter put me in touch for the first time in my adult life with a deep, gnawing sense of being unwanted, unaccepted, unwelcome, and unworthy. I had not *consciously* experienced that menace in many years. It registered now as profound pain. I found myself soaking up the affirmation implicit in their interest like a withered plant soaking up fresh water. It felt so incredibly good to be wanted like this. For some reason awareness of my own feelings and need got through to me.

I had forgotten the pain of my early years in Lake Wobegon, and the awful feelings as a little boy of never being good enough, always being second-rate, always sensing that something was wrong—at school, in town, and at home. Achievement in music and academics from junior high school on had patched those feelings over with "success." But on this day my feelings did an end run on all that intervening "achievement." The affirmation of these students reconnected me powerfully to a deep conviction of being unloved and unlovable. This deep need for affirmation I had not acknowledged was apparently still very present in my adult doings.

Later reflection revealed the surprising number of ways that buried pain played havoc with my attempts to live in love. My family and a trusted colleague helped me see how prominently apology and self-depreciation laced my speech, simultaneously deprecating myself and asking for others to reassure me of my worth after all. Family Renewal work laid bare my penchant for "planning to fail," procrastination, and overcommitment designed to confirm the *"no good, no good"* chant of my inner voice. Even uglier, my control and put-down of those dearest to me seemed also to have ties to my own inner need.

All of this transpired with a person intellectually well aware since childhood that "God so loved the world that he gave his only Son" (John 3:16). I learned it as a lad in Sunday school, studied it as an adult in college and seminary, and ministered to others in light of this affirmation. But, it turns out, the theological affirmation that "God loves me" and the personal awareness that I am loved and worthy of love are two different things.

In Ephesians 5:1–2 Paul points disciples to life grounded in the confidence that they are well-loved children of God. In so doing he challenges the feelings and experiences that undermine our appropriation of this reality and suggests a profoundly healthy and rewarding journey.

The Teaching

Therefore, become imitators of God,
as well loved children,
and live love, as the Messiah loved us
and gave himself for us,
a sacrificial offering to God,
a "pleasing fragrance," as Moses said,
rising from the altar to God (AOT).

The discipleship-recovery journey "from abandoned waif to well-loved child" anchors Paul's amazing instruction. Perhaps it climaxes it all. In fact, the two chief agendas of the journey which bracket the insight-packed paragraph (4:25–5:2) appear to anchor the journey. These chief agendas are: the confrontation of the delusion pervading human fallenness (4:25), and the consciousness of love out of which we might give ourselves to God and others in authentic love (5:1–2). The opening "therefore" in 5:1 signals that this concluding instruction cannot stand alone, but flows out of the preceding truths.

As we saw in the Bible database, these "bracket teachings" state generally the issues addressed specifically in the intervening verses. Negative specifics come under study: destructive anger, parasitic life, toxic talk, rampage rage. Positive alternatives emerge: motivating dynamic, partnership life, constructive communication, tenderheartedness. But in all these negative and positive specifics the issues of thorough integrity and authentic love appear. This strand of the journey explicitly picks up the language of our destiny of holy love from Ephesians 1:4 and points us directly to it.

Unlike the preceding instructions, this one moves directly to positive encouragement, leaving us to infer "the lie" to be put aside in this quest. It assumes the picture of God as Father and invites disciples to image that Father in their own life of love (5:1). This apparently simple instruction broaches, of course, the whole astounding claim that God can be seen as love at all, and especially through the "Father" prism. If true, this understanding of God must displace the skewed pictures of God which shackle the church and the world. Correlative to Paul's exhortation stands the profound biblical teaching that human destiny involves imaging its Creator.

In the most tender moment of the 4:25–5:2 lines, Paul evokes the picture of a precious, well-loved child to present the key stance from which our destiny of holy love will emerge. This picture calls into question all the tragic images that all God's children, and abandoned children in particular, carry from their survival in a fallen world.

Then, building on the distinctively Christian insights received from the life of "The Beloved One" Himself, Messiah Jesus, Paul points to Messiah's own self-giving love as the pattern for ours, the specific shape with which we may approach being "imitators of God" (5:2). The lines climax with the vision put before us of presenting our entire lives to God as an offering, pleasing to Him and profoundly fulfilling to us.

Imitate the Father's Love

"Therefore, become imitators of God, as well-loved children" (5:1). Here Paul sets the compass of the discipleship-recovery journey at its most critical "home" mark. Pointing disciples past worthy models in the church, including Paul himself (1 Cor. 11:1), the apostle lifts our eyes to God Himself as the model, par excellence, for our lives. Knowing we are not God or called to become God, Paul probes the mystery that our destiny entails *imaging* God in select ways.[1]

The Radical Notion of the Divine Father's Love

The idea that God is love weaves through the entire fabric of Ephesians as one of its most important threads. God's kindness and grace, prominent throughout chapters 1 and 2, exhibit His "very great love" (2:4, 7). The entire project of rescuing persons from the penalty and power of sin showcases precisely God's great love. Love, along with peace and faith, come from God, mediated through persons (6:23). Ephesians 5:1–2 clearly implies that Messiah's love most accurately of all reflects the love of God (cf. 3:19; 5:25).

Both in Paul's world and in ours this claim that God is love is radical and hotly debated. Theological inquiry in Paul's world projected highly ambivalent and contradictory pictures of God among the gods of the various major pantheons. Murderous villainy and capricious chaos stand side by side with "love" as chief descriptors of God. Such god concepts still claim the faith of millions of modern persons of non-Christian faiths.

These visions of God expose the problem of finding God at all in the cosmos. Built by reasoning from human experience in the cosmos, the polytheistic pantheons highlight the fact that our experience of nature and history leaves us with ambiguous data from which to form an idea of God. Theologians from Pascal to Pannenberg emphasize that God is the Question No. 1 of human experience. If the reality of God in the cosmos were crystal clear, unmistakably present, the question would not be so widely debated by sincerely seeking, thoughtful persons.

We cannot come to conviction beyond any question that God is, to say nothing of the fact that He is love, *solely* on the basis of our experience of the world. As the writer of Ecclesiastes succinctly put it: "If God is God, then of course we are all in his hands. But whether he loves or hates us, we do not know" (Eccles. 9:1, my paraphrase). Debates about this surface in biblical revelation itself, and form one of the liveliest and most important "canonical conversations" found in Scripture.[2]

Scripture says this question can only be resolved by the revelation of God Himself in history, not by unassisted human reasoning *from* history. Scripture further points us to God's saving acts in history, expounded by God's Spirit, as the primary exhibits of His love (Deut. 7:8–11; Ezek. 16:3–14), and finally claims that at the cross of Jesus this love finds its clearest expression (Rom. 5:8; 8:31–39; 1 John 4:7–12). In Ephesians 5:2, Paul's critical reach to Messiah as the pattern of love we are invited to emulate reflects this faith.

Paul's radical claim confronts not only the problem of discerning God and His character from history, but the problem of every human's experience in a fallen world as well. We are faced not only with the ambiguity of history but also with impairment exaggerated by our experience in fallen families. As we have repeatedly seen, no "perfect families" appear in our world. Families range along a spectrum from consistently dysfunctional and highly destructive to consistently functional and highly nurturing, but none are flawless. No one comes through childhood unscathed.[3]

The role of parents in providing a child's primary pictures of God presents the critical data. Living in a fallen world means not simply that we grow up alienated from God. It also means that we grow up with pictures of God distorted to some degree by the fractured mirrors in which we first saw Him. For some persons these primal pictures of God, stamped deep on our hearts, carry relatively minor distortions which will yield easily to instruction and nurture in faith. Others carry in their hearts such gross caricatures of the living God, the Father of our Lord Jesus, that only persistent instruction and loving support on the discipleship-recovery journey can bring them into conformity with God as He is.

Distorted Deities

Sandra Wilson summarizes these "distorted deities" along five lines:

- The cruel and capricious God.
- The demanding and unforgiving God (more neglect and emotional/verbal abuse than physical abuse).
- The selective and unfair God (who isn't "cruel, capricious, demanding, and unforgiving with all His children—only with them").
- The distant and unavailable God (from chronic parental unavailability).
- The kind but confused God.[4]

Curt Cloninger's video *God-views* puts flesh and blood to these deity distortions. He portrays the Sheriff God, the Butler

God, the Party God, the Cosmic Mechanic God, the God in a Box, and finally the Geriatric God (who falls asleep while working a crossword puzzle and trying to think of a three-letter word for deity!).[5]

So the invitation to imitate God raises the question of what God to imitate and initiates the quest to become aware of the pictures of God we have carried into the discipleship journey.

Human Destiny: Imaging a Holy God in Love

In two closely related passages here, Paul again picks up the question of human destiny he had raised in 1:4 and links it with imaging God. Ephesians 1:4 sketched human destiny as being "holy and blameless before God in love." On the one hand, Paul picks up the "holy" issue. He introduces the habits of holy love (4:25–5:2) as expositions of being "created according to the *likeness of God* in true righteousness and *holiness*" (4:24, emphasis added). Now he calls disciples to imitate God in love (5:2). This theme of human destiny involving the reflection of God Himself is central to biblical thought.

The Bible opens with an essay on creation, Genesis 1:1–2:4. It introduces the book of Genesis and now by canonical placement launches the whole biblical revelation. It's basic, to put it mildly! Genesis 1:27 says:

> *So God created humankind in his image, in the image of God he created them; male and female he created them (NRSV).*

Not their specific sexuality itself—that is, neither maleness nor femaleness itself—but the race's creation in community as male and female images the Creator. Don Joy has shown how this communal imaging of God in our lives as male and female guides us all the way from conception in the womb to consummation in glory.[6]

From this point in Genesis, chapter 1 on, writers add various lines to the theme. In the Pentateuch, God's people are called to be holy because *He* is holy (e.g., Lev. 19:2), an awareness reflected in the famous scene of Isaiah's encounter with God in the Temple

(Isa. 6:1–5). The logic of the book of Jonah assumes God intends His prophet to reflect His own mercy for even the enemies of Israel (cf. Jon. 4:1–11). Elsewhere Paul describes believers as persons who, "seeing the glory of the Lord as though reflected in a mirror, are being transformed into the same image from one degree of glory to another; for this comes from the Lord, the Spirit" (2 Cor. 3:18). The Son of God Himself most clearly images God (Heb. 1:1–4), but the idea lies close at hand in the concept of discipleship itself—following this Imaging One. The book of Ephesians specifies this imaging as the life of holy love.

What biblical revelation proposes, creation data confirms. If this life of holy love does indeed constitute our destiny, it *should* "work" best. "Holy love" should describe life the way it was meant to be lived in any culture at any time. Among many witnesses, C. F. Midelfort's pioneering work at Adolf Gundersen Medical Foundation in LaCrosse, Wisconsin, underscored this "fit." His work confirmed the premise "that learning, growing, maturing, and being well depend on giving and receiving love." He discovered that "the catalyst" promoting the development of healthy relationships in which "persons relate to each other to accomplish a social, cultural, and individual purpose is love."[7]

If human destiny really does center around such things as imaging the Creator, then our journeys are much informed. Our quests for power, status, fame, fortune, and conquest fall miserably short. No wonder they leave us so empty. But neither is self-actualization itself the value sought in discipleship or spiritual quest. The journey is about reflecting the Living God Himself.

Lloyd H. Ahlem's "little" book, *Do I Have to Be Me?*, expounds this truth so beautifully. Exposing the absolute need of human beings for love from the studies of marasmic[8] children and then from our developmental sequence, Ahlem continues by tracing unfolding human destiny in the "experience of agape love." By this he means "to receive and repeat the loving acts of God."[9] From this foundation he shows that exactly in this experience of holy love human beings find a sense of adequacy, validation, authenticity. They find their need to be expended for self-identity and for worship fully met. They enjoy redemptive relationships with themselves and others and develop profound well-being and security.

This is good news indeed, and precisely what Paul's instructions in the discipleship-recovery journey are about.

Key Stance: Well-Loved Child

The phrase "as well-loved children" describes the stance from which disciples imitate God. These critical words make all the difference in the world. They separate endlessly driven religious striving from liberating, fulfilling relationship with the living God; life on a spiritual treadmill from life on "the Way." They separate life with the Sheriff God or Butler God from life with the Loving Father.

More than any other phase of the journey this stance of the "well-loved child" pierces to the very heart of the adult child's problems—indeed to all "children's" problems. "Well-loved" or "beloved" (NRSV) translates a rich word with powerful associations. God used this word to describe His Son, Jesus (Matt. 3:17). This word describes Isaac, Abraham's treasured son (Gen. 22:2, 12, 16). It describes persons particularly dear to others, sometimes, as in Isaac's case, having unique relationship to a parent. It's a rich, warm word for a marvelous relationship.

Core shame spells "not loved," stamped in boldface letters across our hearts. Induced in little ones by physical and emotional abandonment and reinforced by development in dysfunctional families, this "being wound," as Bradshaw calls it, hampers efforts right and left to live in love. Setting aside the lie of one's worthlessness and unlovedness, and accepting—indeed soaking up—the love of God for us in Messiah releases disciples to imitate their Father.

"Children" Implies God as "Father." Describing disciples of Jesus as "children" does imply God as "Father," not because they have been "fathered" by Him but because of the loving relationship they have with Him—or better, the loving relationship *He has with them!* Of the possible names for God other than "God," "Father" predominates in the book of Ephesians (1:2, 3, 17; 2:18; 3:14; 4:6; 6:23). As elsewhere in Scripture, including its use as "Father of our Lord Jesus," "Father" refers to social not sexual realities. God as Father pictures the carrying, providing, loving Providence of the Almighty—reflecting the affection, love, power,

and unchallenged authority of the fathers of the clan or extended families in ancient Israel. Scripture rarely appropriates the "Fatherhood" of God to describe human origins, i.e., does not explore "God the Father" as procreator of children.[10]

For this reason, among others, refraining from calling God "Father" or adopting the heresy of God as "Mother" will not adequately respond to legitimate concerns the church has for women abused by their fathers or other men. No question exists that women *and men* abused by their fathers or other male caregivers frequently have hurdles to surmount in learning to trust themselves to God as Father. But God as Mother poses no less barrier to human worship than God as Father. Human mothers figure as prominently, if not more prominently, as fathers in inducing core shame with its lamentable trail of destruction. In tinkering with God language at this point we have only exchanged one problem for another, and in the process jettisoned the particularity of God's revelation in time (as Father—not as mother or grandfather; to a Son—not to a daughter or nephew; as a Jew—not a German or a New Guinean; in Nazareth—not in Naples or New Orleans, etc.).[11]

The answer here, as in all of the other phases of the discipleship-recovery journey, is learning, growing, healing, freedom. Precisely to *this* particular growth the key stance of the well-loved child invites us.

Appropriating Love We Did Not Know

We find the stance of the "well-loved child" by appropriating for ourselves now the love we never knew. We can come to feel like well-loved children, even if we didn't grow up that way! The needs of the "adult child" can never again be met as a child, for that time is gone forever.[12] But they can be met as an adult, by appropriating love present to us.

We appropriate love we did not know by changing belief systems. Remembering the distorted reality of a fallen world, and particularly the world of adult children, we allow the truth of God to rectify distortions about ourselves and our world. We accept truths like these:

- Jesus died for me, too (Eph. 1:3–14)!

- God shows His great love for me by addressing my most fundamental problem—my alienation from Him, myself, and others—not by healing my cancer or providing prosperity (2:1–10).

- No matter what I've done, God loves me and cares for me too (2:1–10).

- There's always hope (1:15–22). I'm not hopeless!

- I was right! The craziness of my home *was* a dead-end street (4:17–19; 5:3–14).

- God has drawn a circle and included me *in* it (2:11–22).

- The people trying to love me at church aren't being "hokey" or phony; they're actually doing God's will (4:15–16).

- What happened to me wasn't God's idea. He hates it when people are hurt and their worlds turn dark and dull (5:3–14).

- God has great plans for me because He loves me (1:3–14).

These truths can replace the destructive "self-talk" that dins self-hate and failure at the shame-based soul. They displace "The Voice,"[13] as Firestone calls this self-indicting, continually stuck, internal record. They fill that track with the comfort of God's love.

Accepting love God gives us through others also allows us to appropriate love we never knew. The church's "body language" is God's gift of love to us. We can experience the love of the Father through other persons in the fellowship who *do* live love, who *do* feel loved, and who do authentically care about us (4:15–16). Remember, we are learning boundaries and learning to tell the truth about ourselves and others. This involves not just "the church" of our time and place, but also accepts love mediated through saints of other places and times. Through hymns our hearts are opened to God's love. Through biography, history, and other literature we sense the love of God through persons who have known it. So we stop the put-offs and wall-building that isolate us from intimacy, that shut off the flow of genuine love and affirmation from others.

We learn to feel like well-loved children even if we didn't grow up that way by speaking the truth about ourselves. Already noted, we stop "the lie" that perpetuates our sense of isolation, unworthiness, unlovedness. We can stop flippant apology for ourselves and our work. Stop discounting the value and importance of who we are and what we do. Stop the toxic self-talk. Learn to speak well of ourselves, apply Scripture's famous lines to ourselves (e.g., 1 Cor. 13)! This mounts no call for boasting or grandiosity. No, we simply speak the truth about ourselves, including our growth, our accomplishments, our achievements, our plans, as well as our failures and needs.

Taking care of ourselves fosters a sense of being well-loved and actually opens us up to the love of God and others. To some this may seem like trading self-hate for self-worship and selfishness. Persons particularly inundated with hate talk from "The Voice" need time for special focus on themselves, but this would not chart their discipleship path forever. Sandra Wilson likens this to the focus on an ankle during care for a bad sprain, and then comments: "Normally we do not live ankle-focused lives."[14] As we have already seen, the discipleship-recovery journey leads to authentic care for others, as well as ourselves. But one stop on the journey that cannot be omitted without damage is *learning* to care for ourselves. Learning to steward the gift God has given us is the point (5:15–16).

Opening to God's Spirit also enables us to appropriate love we have not known and to feel well loved, even if we did not grow up that way. Through God's Spirit His love has been "poured out into our hearts" (Rom. 5:5). God's Spirit speaks deep assurance to us that we are God's children (Rom. 8:16–17) and actually enables us to cry out to God, "Abba! Father!" (Rom. 8:15). God works through the structures of human personality and social order He has made, so we can expect His Spirit to speak love to us through the very means we have just considered. God also works through His creation, accomplishing His purposes in ways that exceed our capacity to understand (Eph. 1:11–12; 3:20–21). We open by prayer, meditation, and obedience to the Spirit who brings forth in our lives the marks that exhibit our authentic relationship with God (1:14).

Take Chief Clues From Messiah

Paul puts a distinctively Christian spin on the idea of imitating God by directing us to the life of Messiah as our example. Back to discipleship—i.e., following Jesus—again!

Authentic Self-Giving

Messiah "gave Himself up for us," Paul says (Eph. 5:2), and notes this as the expression of love most worthy of our emulation. This can involve "giving ourselves *to*" others in true intimacy, sharing our thoughts and feelings and selves. But it means more. "Giving ourselves *up for*" others marks a stage of the discipleship journey where the problems that plague adult children have been squarely faced.

Adult children confuse love with pity, and are drawn to needy persons to which and for which to give themselves. They do this not because of genuine love, but because of their own inner need to be wanted and needed and superior to another. As we saw in Chapter 8, this just puts a thin disguise on a parasitic life. In this mode we often give ourselves away before we have taken possession of ourselves. We may even ask if in these behaviors we really do give *ourselves* up, for others are in reality making our choices for us. This does not mean all martyrdom or sacrifice of oneself exposes personal problems. As a matter of fact, actualizing our destiny of holy love must eventually involve the capacity and willingness to give ourselves up for others.

Genuine "giving up" oneself for others arises, as it did in the life of Jesus, from the strength of the well-loved child (cf. John 3:35; 15:9; 17:24, 26). John 13:1–3 paints this as clearly as any scene in the New Testament. Note how the famous "towel and basin" chapter opens. John introduces Jesus as the one who knew who He was, where He was, where He was going, what strength and authority He had, what resources belonged to Him, and what difficulty He faced. *This* Messiah—well-loved by the Father—rose from the table, took the towel and washed the disciples' feet as an introduction to His passion (John 13:4 ff.)!

As in the Gospels, giving ourselves up for others can mean literally offering our lives for another or giving ourselves up in loving relationships day by day. The invitation to discipleship in the

Gospels carried the same breadth of meaning. "Take up their cross" meant disciples could face literal Roman crosses as their Master was about to do (Mark 8:34). More fundamentally, it meant learning to think like God and His Messiah (8:31–33). This Messiah-thinking meant opening to others, accepting little children, giving up manipulation and abuse of others, finding life in following Jesus as opposed to less worthy and temporary goals, and so on. (Read the pictures in Mark 9:2–10:52.) So also in Ephesians, this "gave himself up for us" life takes the shape of loving relationships with spouses, children, servants, and masters (Eph. 5:22–6:9).

Life as an Offering to God

Just as authentic self-giving meets a deep "need to be expended," as Lloyd Ahlem says, doing it as life offered to God meets the "need to worship."[15] Paul uses language familiar to readers of the Hebrew Scriptures in his day, quoting God's words through Moses about Israel's offerings to God. The offering by fire would rise as a "pleasing odor to the Lord," says Leviticus (1:9, 13, 17, etc.). Describing our loving imitation of God as a sacrificial offering, a pleasing fragrance to God, Paul transforms our walk into worship.

Here we come home to God—really. Here we find the center around which a truly human life can emerge. This is because the codependent, addictive life of adult children actually constitutes idolatry—the worship of alien gods, says Bradshaw.

Co-dependence is core addiction. It is a diseased form of life. Once a person believes that his identity lies outside himself in a substance, activity, or another person, *he has found a new god, sold his soul and become a slave* [Bradshaw's emphasis].[16]

Our whole existence is brought under this rubric, enabling us to integrate our entire lives around the worship of the Father. As Paul phrased it in Colossians 3:17: "And *whatever* you do, in word or deed, do in the name of the Lord Jesus, *giving thanks to God the Father through him*" (emphasis added).

Our lives themselves—freed to love and be loved, to receive and give ourselves away—become a symphony of praise to the Father.

Here we come home to God . . . *From Abandoned Waif to Well-Loved Child.*

Questions for Reflection

1. Do I have reason to think the abuse I experienced at the hands of my father or mother is thwarting my desire to trust myself to God?

2. Do I seem driven to give to others, to sacrifice for others, as though more by some alien compulsion than by the leading of Messiah's Spirit?

3. Do I often wind up disillusioned in my sacrifice, feeling cheated and not appreciated, as though what I really seek is some inner payoff, not the free living of my destiny of holy love?

4. Have I accepted inadequate, God-language solutions to my deeper need to learn to live as a well-loved child?

5. Do I shut out God's love to me by blocking the nurture and love others would like to give me in Jesus' name?

6. Do I block the truth by staying with my self-destructive "Voice," and thereby also block a sense of being loved?

7. Do I compartmentalize my life, putting some parts in a "sacred" or "religious" box and others in a "secular" or "regular" box, and thus prevent entering a truly integrated life with God?

8. Do I need to take time to focus on caring for myself in order that I may accept the Father's love and learn to care for others?

9. Have I gotten stuck in my "ankle focus"? Have I become fixated in preoccupation with myself in the name of "recovery"?

10. Knowing what I now know of who I am and where I came from, have I offered—do I offer—my whole self up to God as a symphony of praise to Him?

Questions
and Reflections

The widespread challenge to Christian appropriation of psychological "insights" and serious reservation about the "recovery movement" in particular are well known. Significant questions arise that we do not want to sidestep.

Are the "Twelve Steps" Christian?

Our description of the discipleship-recovery journey has been only loosely tied to the Twelve Steps (see Addendum for complete list of the Twelve Steps). Nevertheless, at several points we have indicated common ground and have taken a generally sympathetic stance to their use.

Are the Twelve Steps really Christian then? No. But they only make *theological* sense within a Judeo-Christian framework. As we saw, the Twelve Steps were incubated in the evangelical Christian influences of the Oxford Group and Episcopalian Sam Shoemaker. But they were "hatched" by AA founder Bill Wilson as a deliberately non-sectarian, spiritual program open to all faiths and even persons of no faith.[1] AA set its goal solely on attaining and retaining sobriety and definitely not on Christian discipleship.

Thus the Twelve Steps speak of a "Power greater than ourselves" (Step 1) and "God *as we understood Him*" (Step 3). Here we meet the "Higher Power" of the general Recovery movement, and not the Covenant God of Israel or "The God and Father of Our Lord."

But, although the Twelve Steps are themselves not specifically Christian, neither are they *anti*-Christian. Much depends on the context and mode of their use. The logic of the Twelve Steps is Judeo-Christian, beginning with their concept of God. Taken at face value they assume a God:

- Other than oneself who wills and acts, i.e., a "personal being"
- Able and willing to interact redemptively with human beings, helping to bring their unmanageable lives under control, reforming their character, responding to their prayer
- Whose character defines good and evil in such ways that abuses to human beings and their relationships, like those encountered in alcoholism, are regarded as "defects" to be removed
- To whose "care" one could entrust oneself and could do so without fear
- Who relates to human beings essentially in authentic trust relationship
- Who sustains moral accountability and fosters confession and the making of amends
- Of universal, cross-cultural significance so that one would take this "message" to others and invite others (presumably all who will) to live by the principles of the Twelve Steps

So far as I am aware, the deities of Hinduism, Buddhism, Shintoism, Islam, and other world religions do not fit this profile, and neither does New Age ideology. Even modern Judaism with its emphatically non-proselytizing God stumbles on the last point.

"Power greater than ourselves" or "God as we understand him" construed as the cosmic life force, the group itself, or simply as a dependent stance toward "nothing out there" may indeed produce change in persons. But it cannot survive the test of theological consistency. In spite of this, God in mercy often mediates His grace to needy persons through these inadequate channels. For this reason some Christians understandably continue to use these inadequate words to cast the net as widely as possible in outreach, in the hope of overt Christian ministry later (the "Acts 17" approach).

But heavy traces of Judeo-Christian theology reside in the logic of the steps. Careful reflection on the implications of what one is saying in these affirmations leads easily to the God and Father of Jesus, who alone fits the God assumed in the Twelve Steps and more. Easily edited to an explicitly Christian discipleship-recovery journey or used in a Christian context, they "work" best, most consistently and open to exposition in the hands of disciples of Jesus.

Why have you talked so much about alcoholics and drug addicts and their families? I still don't see what that has to do with me and my family.

This important question stands near the center of what this whole inquiry is about. Two reasons make our references to these seriously addicted persons understandable. First, alcoholics/drug addicts and their families exhibit on a large and dramatic scale the sorts of problems found to a lesser degree in "normal" families. The tragedy of these families allows us to see clearly the delusion and skewed thinking, the inappropriate anger, the toxic talk, the parasitic ways, numbed-out feelings, and lack of authentic love also present in less troubled families (albeit more subtly). These severely stressed families where addiction distorts reality put, if you will, a magnifying glass on family relationships, exaggerating and uncovering the dynamics present less starkly in other families. Looking at them we get clues for the sorts of things, good and bad, to look for in less troubled families—the sorts of things we think we may have.

Second, this population has received significant, extended attention since just before the Second World War. Thousands of families have been helped and studied, generating a wealth of insight on the nature of human families. Aggressive attention to alcoholism and drug addiction has afforded the opportunity to learn much about family interaction and development. From this and other troubled populations we have learned much about the sorts of family relationships that sustain life, and also about those which injure and destroy persons. We ignore that wisdom to our hurt.

How does the discipleship-recovery journey relate to "sanctification" and "entire sanctification" (or "the deeper life" or "the Spirit-filled life")?

The short answer is this: the "discipleship-recovery journey" is "sanctification" and "sanctification" *is* "the discipleship-recovery journey." That is, discipleship-recovery and sanctification, using different language, deal with many of the same issues. Both focus ultimately on the development of persons characterized by authentic love here and now. Both discipleship-recovery and sanctification provide specific, meaningful content to holy love. They help us understand what living in holy love is actually all about. These are not simply matters of *personal* development, because they relate to living love. Since living love is a moral and spiritual issue for Christians, "recovery" agendas are a matter not simply of "development" or "maturation" but of "sanctification."

"Sanctification" names the process whereby God's people are transformed into the image of Christ, the grace by which they are made increasingly like the Master. Sanctification relates not to the forgiveness of our "sins" (our acts of sin) but to our being cleansed from "sin" (from our enthronement of self). This "sin," this "enthronement of self" Paul calls "the flesh," referring not to our "flesh and blood, skin and bones" but to a way of thinking and living governed by fallen human desire. Traditional doctrinal terms "carnal" and "carnality" denote this thought and life. This "flesh" Paul contrasts to "the mind of Christ," "the mind on the Spirit," and to "life according to the Spirit" (cf. 1 Cor. 2:13–3:4; Rom. 8:1–11).

Negatively, the sanctification process involves reorientation of ourselves away from the enthronement of self. Positively the sanctification journey involves reorientation of ourselves to the will and love of Christ. Scripture calls this reorientation of our person away from self-enthronement the "cleansing" or "purifying" of the "heart" from sin (the "heart" naming us as persons that think, commit, decide, feel, evaluate, etc.). The reorientation of ourselves *to* the will and love of Christ Scripture describes, among other ways, as "the renewing of your minds" (Rom.12:1–2); "being renewed in the spirit of your minds" (Eph. 4:23); "putting on the new person, created after God's image in righteousness and true holiness" (Eph. 4:24). If one were forced to isolate the feature most pervasively characteristic of this process it would surely be the emergence of wholehearted, authentic, holy love for God, for others and for oneself.[2] Writers in the "recovery" community recognize the development of authentic love as the chief agenda of recovery as well.[3]

"*Entire* sanctification" describes a relationship with God in which God's people live oriented around, focused on, governed by the love of Christ—thoroughly, completely, consistently. In Bible terms (AOT) they are "cleansed from *all* sin" (1 John 1:9), they "live *full* of the Spirit," (Eph. 5:18), they "walk according to Christ's Spirit" (Rom. 8:4).

"Entire sanctification" addresses the spiritual and often personal ambivalence which commonly surfaces in Christian experience as persons set out to walk with the Lord. This spiritual ambivalence Paul saw in the Corinthian Christians whom he said on the one hand were genuine followers of Jesus (1 Cor. 1:1–9), but on the other hand harbored values and thoughts much like their pagan neighbors (1 Cor. 3:1–4). The issue is not that these persons continually and regularly succumb to temptation and continue living in sin. The New Testament clearly affirms that persons truly born of God do *not* continue controlled by sin and do not regularly suffer defeat in temptation (1 John 3:7–10; Rom. 6:1–14). Nor is the issue that Jesus now becomes their Lord, while before He was simply their Savior, for the confession "Jesus is Lord" sets the baseline for *all* Christians (Rom. 10:9–10; 1 Cor. 12:1–3). Rather, the central issue in their spiritual ambivalence is these Christians' incapacity in living out the life of love to which Christ calls them. This inability regularly to "walk in love," as Paul put it in Ephesians 5:1–2, in turn hinges on the issue of self-centeredness, self-enthronement.

The core of Christian discipleship finds expression in at least two powerful ways in the New Testament: 1) the New Covenant's "new" command that we love one another as Jesus loved us (John 13:34), and 2) the straightforward call to every single prospective disciple to follow Jesus to the Cross (Mark 8:34–9:1). Both of these expressions cut directly to life's main agenda—the surrender of our entire selves to God, the issue of literally giving our whole selves to Christ. They go beyond forgiveness of sins and separation from God to the deeper issue of our whole life orientation. They address the core allegiance which organizes our values, thoughts, and commitments, and which directs our behavior.

The ambivalence develops as believers set out to follow Jesus to the Cross and begin to live with their Lord's "simple" instruction to love others as He loved them. They continually bump into a startling realization! The call to love as Jesus loved repeatedly asks them to give themselves away, to set aside their own preferences for the well-being of another, to choose not simply in their own interest but with the interest of others in mind as well, and so on.

God resolves this ambivalence by orienting the believer's heart around the love of Christ through the power of the Spirit. The realities which were in principle theirs from the beginning of their walk with Christ now, in fact, actually and decisively emerge. In biblical language, they are now actually done with the "old person" which they put away in principle at conversion (Col. 2:9–17; Eph. 4:22–24). The fullness of the Spirit into which they were baptized they now actually live (Eph. 5:18 ff.). The resurrection life to which they were joined when they were "buried with Christ" they now actually express consistently (Rom. 6:1–14; 8:1–17). In the language of the prayer we studied in Ephesians, chapter 3, these persons are now actually "rooted and grounded in love" (Eph. 3:17).

Just as important, this resolution of our fundamental ambivalence of allegiance with its accompanying roots and foundations in love is in important aspects just a beginning. It is *the door to growth in grace* on a new level, accelerated and enhanced by wholehearted surrender. This resolution is the gateway to "comprehend[ing], with all saints, what is the breadth and length and height and depth" of Christ's love (Eph. 3:18). God enables us to pursue on a new level and to new lengths and depths the implications of both His love *for us* and His *love through us* to others.

In spite of the joy and victory of this life, this growth in grace proves a tremendous challenge, filled frequently with intense spiritual struggle, and even at times defeat. Temptation for all human beings, including the entirely sanctified, is always *real temptation* to sin, never simply an abstraction. Human beings, including the entirely sanctified, are always capable of sin. (Remember Adam?) And human sin is immensely complex and multifaceted. These facts among others guarantee the journey for *all believers* will always constitute actual growth, real battle, as well as true joy and victory.

This reality of life "rooted and grounded" in love which Wesleyans call "entire sanctification" is no peculiar possession of the Wesleyan tradition or sectarian emphasis of the holiness movement. Happily, the life thus rooted in Messiah's presence is the common treasure of the church universal.[4] Considerable confusion obscures this common heritage, however, because different traditions describe this experience with different language, depending mainly on their understanding of sin. In addition, qualities which *all* commonly figure into this reality find differing accent in one or another of the traditions—increased spiritual power for life and witness, enhanced assurance, increased love. This adds further to the variety in expectation and description believers encounter in preaching and teaching. Again, the ongoing *process* of sanctification on the one hand and the crises of surrender and faith, which move Christian growth in grace along on the other, receive differing emphasis.

How does "discipleship-recovery" clarify the business of "growth in grace" or "spiritual growth" or "spiritual formation"?

Discipleship-recovery clarifies the business of growth in grace in at least two important ways. First, discipleship-recovery elaborates specific components of "holy love."

Growth in grace, spiritual growth—the whole sanctification process—is essentially about growth in holy love. But even *agape* "love" needs definition. How would we know "growth in holy love" when we saw it? What specific goals of spiritual growth would we have in mind to mark the process of "growing in love"? We have used two resources to answer these questions: biblical revelation and recovery literature.

Biblical Pictures of Holy Love

As we have seen, biblical pictures of holy love such as that found in the book of Ephesians explore areas such as these:

- Profound integrity
- Recovery of reality about intergenerational human relationships
- Redemptive anger
- Appropriate inner and outer boundaries
- Accountability and self-responsibility
- Development beyond dependence and independence to inter-dependence
- Communication habits that level, liberate, redeem
- Recovery of full-spectrum feeling, including compassion and tenderness
- Authentic forgiveness
- Authentic self-giving

These are all patterned after the image of Jesus Messiah. Growth in these matters *is* growth in love. Understandings of "love" that do not take into account these agendas prove inadequate.

The recovery literature clarifies just how these virtues and their absence figure in the development of families and the people in them. The specific sorts of behavior entailed in redemptive communication, for example, or in the development of appropriate boundaries become clear from the families studied in the recovery movement.

Second, discipleship-recovery gives meaning to "the sins of the sanctified"—even those of the entirely sanctified. The personal and family situations addressed by the recovery movement force the conclusion that some of the most destructive human behavior is unintentional. Repeatedly adult children coping with serious damage inflicted on them emotionally and even physically face the fact that their caregivers "meant well" or "did the best they knew." In many cases and without conscious plan, their parents constructed homes perpetuating the same destructive patterns of relationship they themselves had known as children (often declaring all the while they would never be like their parents!). Their parents' intentions, good or otherwise, do not change what these children actually experienced. Their parents' lack of knowledge or lack of awareness as to what was actually happening in their home does not mitigate the ensuing damage. This situation underscores the complex nature of human choice, motivation, and accountability.

This proves particularly true when we deal with "the law of love" and with the various character traits entailed in holy love (as noted above). How persons become tangled in the webs of delusion that we probed in chapter 6 is very complex, involving multiple choices spanning generations. How anger gets nurtured and transferred, as we saw in chapter 7, does not yield to simple answer. How various toxic patterns of speech that destroy others are learned, how our boundaries become damaged and our regard for the boundaries of others impaired, and so on—how these all occur proves a very complex matter. Rarely do these attitudes and behaviors involve single, simple, clear "transgressions of a known law of God." Instead they involve complex patterns of choice with widely divergent levels of accountability. They involve choices made across generational and family boundaries. They include patterns learned before one was even aware of the process. Nevertheless, it is precisely these habits, through which we are damaged, by which we then hurt and even destroy others.

Perhaps most crucial for Christian families, recovery data exposes the fact that the socially acceptable compulsions and addictions prove as destructive to families as the more odious ones. The various socially approved ways in which persons manipulate and control others prove just as poisonous to families as the manipulation and control built into alcoholism and other substance abuse. Recovery data unmasks behaviors generally accepted, sometimes even applauded in the church, for the destructive behaviors they actually are. The approval of these behaviors by our culture, including our church cultures, hides their seriousness from us and keeps us from realizing what we are doing to ourselves and to persons around us.

So the discipleship-recovery study leads us to take much more seriously the biblical category of "unintentional sin" or "inadvertent sin." This is sin occasioned by ignorance or by accident, or sin whose choosing is unclear. Moses' treatment of these "inadvertent sins" in Leviticus, chapter 5, deals with acts relating mainly to matters of worship in ancient Israel. But in the process he opens up a sort of sin worthy of consideration beyond matters of liturgy and worship protocol.

Here we encounter breaches of God's will done accidentally, done in ignorance, some involving forgetfulness (Lev. 5:1, 3, 4, 15, 17). These are considered sin and "breaches of faith" because, in the Leviticus context, often an oath to God is broken in the process. Further reflection uncovers the fact that much inadvertent sin not only poses an insult to God but also injures others. In all such sin, the key is how the offending party responds upon becoming aware of his or her sin. When awareness of the offense leads to confession and reparation, forgiveness proves possible (5:5, 13). Restitution may be involved (5:16).

Important results emerge for persons on the discipleship-recovery journey, particularly for Wesleyan pilgrims. First, they stop hiding behind intention. They do not allow their heritage's helpful emphasis on the purification of motive to block the realization that what they intended in much of their doings with their families may be less important than what they actually said and did. They understand that as a matter of fact human motivation is sufficiently complex, and that determining the precise nature of their motives in many cases will be impossible and often of minimal help.

Second, where warranted they accept Scripture's counsel in calling these failures of ignorance and judgment—these expressions of abandonment, abuse, trauma, and other inner need—"sin," even if inadvertent. They understand that these behaviors may often have injured others and themselves. They call these breaches of God's best will "sin" so as to register the lethal nature of their results for persons around them and consequently their profound seriousness to God. There are indeed simple infirmities and mistakes. They are not moral issues. But the "mistakes" and "errors" that concern us here are too serious not to be called "sin."

Third, they realize the importance of the kind of teaching that makes clear the sorts of acting, speaking, and relating which, though hidden from their awareness, destroy them and others. They pursue insight that will help them become aware of their need and open them to confession and the possibility of change.

They understand that this business of actually learning to live out the love of Christ will be a lifelong task. In all of this, they do not surrender the New Testament's paradoxical but joyful emphasis on deliverance from sin, while at the same time pursuing the ongoing process of being cleansed from all sin as it comes to light.

With all of this emphasis on our hidden needs and the unwitting ways in which we perpetuate the hurt of human fallenness, how can we find any sense of joy and victory in Christ?

As we celebrate the power of God's grace and embrace the paradox of life on the journey, we can be at one and the same time pure in heart and in some sense sinners. The New Testament's accent falls on the power of God's grace truly to deliver us from all sin, truly to raise us to new life, truly to fill us with the mind of Messiah. Viewed from a certain perspective (see our last question), we will be uncovering sin in our lives to our final days. But the gospel's accent is not on our continuing confrontation with sin but on our continuing victory in Christ. Just as John Wesley stressed the optimism of the gospel, so we should put our accent there as well.

Victory comes in trusting to God and His infinite grace all that we are and hope to be. Victory comes in surrendering to God and His unchanging love every last thing we know about ourselves, and also all we do not know. Victory comes in committing ourselves to walk with Christ no matter what the cost or implications. Victory does not rest on the flawlessness of our lives nor on the health or balance of our personality.

God does not seem to cleanse our hearts beyond what we know of our need. The Spirit does not appear to rectify those injuries of our heart, those skewings of our motive, those compulsions of our mind which lie hidden to us. This is true, despite the fact that these hidden problems often compromise significantly our capacity to actualize consistently the wholehearted surrender we have genuinely made to Christ.

If this observation is correct—that God does not seem to cleanse our hearts beyond what we know of our need—it is for reasons of His own. We might wish it otherwise, and might even theorize that it is or must be different. We could insist, for instance, that if entire sanctification means anything at all, then God meets all of our need or He meets none of it. In the face of continuing spiritual struggle, however, this approach leads directly to one of two conclusions: either 1) the person did not surrender all there was to surrender, i.e., didn't trust God completely, or 2) there is no such thing as "full salvation" or "entire sanctification." This all-or-nothing approach sounds robust on the surface, but proves inadequate to describe life as the saints experience it.

Similar difficulties face the "all-or-nothing" approach to divine healing or to release from addiction to alcohol or drugs. Based on individual episodes, persons may claim that if one simply believes with sufficient strength that God will heal, God will deliver you from alcohol or drugs. Cases are then cited to prove that, as a matter of fact, upon occasion God does indeed heal persons outright, does indeed deliver them from long-standing addictions in a single moment of rescue. Unfortunately these instantaneous deliverances prove not to be the only way, perhaps not even the most common way God delivers persons. The same proves true in this matter of the cleansing of our hearts.

This involves the reality that God will address the hidden, "unwitting" facets of our moral and spiritual problems only as they become known to us and surrendered to Him. "General confession" and "general surrender" and "general commitment" are vitally important because they keep us oriented clearly to God's will. But the complex compromises of our walk in love that lie hidden from us will only yield to grace as we become aware of them and give them with insight to Christ. Hence the importance of candid instruction, "real life" discipling, robust truth gathering in the church.

All this explains why significant "growth in grace" is not simply a matter of time or longevity in the Kingdom. Persons can live for decades making repeated and sincere "general surrender" of "all I am and ever hope to be" to God without altering significantly the deeper patterns of relationship which contradict and undermine that intent. For this reason this book has claimed that instruction in our spiritual family heritage, in the many faces of anger, in patterns of communication, in boundary development, and more are not simply matters of "personal" development. They are rather agendas of spiritual growth, of sanctification and discipleship, for without them deep growth eludes us.

So we find victory in focusing primary intent on what we do know, surrendering ourselves wholly to God and not worrying about what we do not know. At the same time we proceed confidently and humbly in uncovering what lies hidden from us. Victory arises as we hold nothing back from God's hand and His Spirit, while asking Him and trusted friends around us to help us learn more and more about ourselves.

In fact, a critical value of "full surrender" is its role in prompting openness to further insight and growth in grace. If we have already settled the issue that we do not have to have our own way, that we do not have to justify ourselves, that we are not loved of God because we are flawless, that we want to be like Jesus more than we want anything else—if we have settled these things, we are much more likely to "walk in the light" that uncovers surprising, unseemly features in our life.

Afterword

In *God's Healing for Hurting Families,* I offered our family's journey as a case study of a hurting family desperately needing God's healing. A new edition of a book like this raises the question of "the rest of the story."

The "absolute rescue from destruction" of which I spoke then in chapter 1 has proven authentic. The new direction our family took by the grace of God and hard work has become indeed a road to a life worth probing, deepening, and pursuing. Since the book's first release, we have faced crises that I think would have destroyed us, had we not been charting our course by a whole new set of assumptions and insights. Our thirty-eighth wedding anniversary provided a marvelous arena for celebrating new life and new love. It was a miracle of grace. Even so, a key realization was yet to dawn.

Further poking in our family tree brought another startling insight. Mental illness was nearly as widespread in our genogram as were toxic modes of family relationships, although the two "maps" did not completely coincide. So as we have continued to work with my own depression, it has become clear that I brought to our marriage not only skewed ideas of "normal" family life but also a genetic predisposition to affective disorders such as major depression and bipolar disorder. With proper medication my depression is quite manageable. This medical help has made it possible to focus spiritual and personal energy on continuing growth in the habits of holy love.

All of this has underscored for me the multifaceted array of influences that converge moment by moment to produce who I am and how I relate to God and to other human beings. Clearly, *mental health* (or mental illness) figures constantly in the mix, just as any other systemic disorders like diabetes or cardiovascular disease would. Thoughts and behaviors are impacted by *environmental conditioning* from primary caregivers, extended family, school, church, work and a host of other associations. This conditioning impinges constantly on who I am and what I do. Even with these influences, however, I remain responsible for my own *awareness and accountability* for what I think, say, and do. Finally, through all of this, the Spirit of God continues to be active in our lives, bringing grace to bear upon us through an infinite number of influences.

It has become increasingly clear that living responsibly in holy love calls for a multifaceted set of responses. Mental illness has to be diagnosed and treated medically and spiritually. (I relate God's healing power to mental illness along the same lines that I relate divine healing to any other illness.) Deeply engrained ways of toxic thinking, doing, and being must be unmasked and unlearned. Habits of holy love must be learned and "put on" daily by the grace of God in brand new circumstances. The work of God's Spirit must be received regularly through Scripture reading and meditation, through fellowship, worship, confession, service, prayer, and other means of grace.

None of this "just happens" without my taking primary responsibility for who I am and what I do. Evading accountability by blaming my parents and my environment changes nothing. It simply perpetuates pain and hurt. Refusing to stay on my medicine because of embarrassment or arguments about whether and how God heals just sabotages healing. Launching into vague God talk about spirituality and growth in grace misses the point without specific insights of holy love in place.

But choosing to work with what God has placed in my hands continues to show great promise. Accepting the healing potential of whatever resources Christ brings to me—spiritual, medical, social, psychological—still fuels profound recovery. Actually comprehending and living out the breadth and the length and the height and the depth of the love of Christ remains a goal worthy of my family's full engagement to the glory of God.

—David L. Thompson
Advent 2003

Addendum

The Twelve Steps

1. We admitted we were powerless over alcohol—that our lives had become unmanageable.
2. Came to believe that a Power greater than ourselves could restore us to sanity.
3. Made a decision to turn our will and our lives over to the care of God *as we understood Him.*
4. Made a searching and fearless moral inventory of ourselves.
5. Admitted to God, to ourselves, and to another human being the exact nature of our wrongs.
6. Were entirely ready to have God remove all these defects of character.
7. Humbly asked Him to remove our shortcomings.
8. Made a list of all persons we had harmed and became willing to make amends to them all.
9. Made direct amends to such people wherever possible, except when to do so would injure them or others.
10. Continued to take personal inventory and when we were wrong promptly admitted it.

11. Sought through prayer and meditation to improve our conscious contact with God *as we understood Him,* praying only for knowledge of His will for us and the power to carry that out.

12. Having had a spiritual awakening as the result of these steps, we tried to carry this message to alcoholics and to practice these principles in all our affairs.

The Twelve Steps are reprinted with permission of Alcoholics Anonymous World Services, Inc. Permission to reprint the Twelve Steps does not mean that A.A. has reviewed or approved the contents of this publication, nor that A.A. agrees with the views expressed herein. A.A. is a program of recovery from alcoholism only—uses of the Twelve Steps in connection with programs and activities which are patterned after A.A., but which address other problems, or in any other non-A.A. context, does not imply otherwise.

Notes

Chapter 1

1. "Adult children," they informed us, were adults driven by the quest to fill the void of unmet childhood needs. These were adults hamstrung by coping mechanisms appropriate to traumatized children but inadequate and even destructive as adult behavior.

2. Bible quotations marked AOT are the author's own translation where they differ from the NRSV, which is followed unless otherwise indicated.

Chapter 2

1. I say "almost as though" because the logic of the entire epistle is not this tightly linked, and because the causal movement from 4:17–24 to 4:25 ff. cannot be extended rigidly back through the whole foregoing section. Nevertheless, there is another sense in which the link is quite appropriate. The apostle has just three paragraphs earlier built his instructional material in general directly on the foundation of 1:3–3:21. He called this his plea for "a life worthy of the calling to which you [the Ephesians] have been called" (4:1). Inasmuch as he now turns to his first particularization of these general exhortations, the force of the transition at 4:1 is very close at hand. So it is not stretching the logic of the work to see the preceding material coming to bear quite forcefully in these exhortations of 4:25–5:2.

2. Kenneth J. Collins emphasizes this root malady and our culture's tendency not to see it in his chapter, "The Root of the Problem," *Soul Care: Deliverance and Renewal Through the Christian Life* (Wheaton, IL: Victor Books, 1995), 13–55.

Chapter 3

1. Frederick Buechner, *Telling Secrets* (San Francisco: Harper & Row, 1989), 104–105.

2. Kenneth Collins elaborates the powerful resources which come to believers through the family of faith under "Disciplines of the Liberated Life" in two chapters of his *Soul Care,* 147–183.

Chapter 4

1. John Bradshaw, *Bradshaw On: The Family, a Revolutionary Way of Self-Discovery* (Deerfield Beach, FL: Health Communications, 1988). As for Bradshaw himself, his own family's history regrettably illustrates the difficulty of appropriating what one knows for one's own benefit. This does not, in my judgment, undermine the validity of his findings.

2. As Bradshaw explains, "Historically the studies in chemically dependent families began to reveal the dysfunctional structure of other types of families. Through studying alcoholism and the alcoholic family, a whole range of compulsive/addictive patterns emerged to explain other dysfunctional families," *Bradshaw On: The Family,* 94. See also Waguish R. Guirguis, "The Family and Schizophrenia," *Psychiatric Annals* 10, no. 7 (July, 1980): 269–275. Guirguis reviews and evaluates the research on schizophrenia and the family by Murray Bowen and Lyman Wynne at the National Institute of Mental Health; Don Jackson, Gregory Bateson, and others at the Mental Health Institute at Palo Alto; Theodore Lidz at Yale; Ronald Laing in Britain.

3. Tim Stafford, "The Therapeutic Revolution," *Christianity Today* 37, no. 6 (May 17, 1993): 24–32, reviews the primary voices in this critique and their main concerns.

4. John G. Howells, "An Overview of Family Psychiatry," *Psychiatric Annals* 10, no. 2 (February, 1980): 40–45, provides an excellent outline of this development. Howells himself was among the pioneers in "family psychiatry." Don D. Jackson and Virginia Satir trace the various developmental strands of the awareness of the family's importance in psychiatric theory and practice, reaching all the way back to 1911 in "A Review of Psychiatric Developments in Family Diagnosis and Family Therapy," pp. 29–51 in *Exploring the Base for Family Therapy* (New York: Family Service Association, 1961), edited by Nathan W. Ackerman, Frances L. Beatman, and Sanford N. Sherman.

5. For much of the story, see *Alcoholics Anonymous: The Story of How Many Thousands of Men and Women Have Recovered from Alcoholism* (New York City: Alcoholics Anonymous Publishing, 1954; first published in 1939). For an overview, including helpful insights regarding the roots of AA in evangelical Christianity, see Tim Stafford's "The Hidden Gospel of the 12 Steps," *Christianity Today* 35, no. 8 (July 22, 1991): 14–19.

6. Giving advice "To Wives" (their major work at the beginning was with men and much of the writing assumes the spouse will be a wife) and to "The Family Afterward," *Alcoholics Anonymous,* 117–149.

7. Some of these interrelationships can be illustrated by "crossovers" between psychiatric treatment of alcohol abuse and the AA programs in the contributors to the book, *Al-Anon Faces Alcoholism* (New York: Al-Anon Family Group Headquarters, Inc., 1965). Contributors included Joan K. Jackson, Ph.D., a sociologist working as Research Associate Professor of Psychiatry at the University of Washington School of Medicine; Ruth Fox, M.D., a practicing psychiatrist and Medical Director of the National Council on Alcoholism; Margaret B. Bailey, D.S.W., Director of Research, National Council on Alcoholism.

8. The balance, stability, or equilibrium sought by the family is known technically as the "homeostasis" of the family system. The concept is traced by Sanford N. Sherman to the work of Nathan W. Ackerman (*A Dynamic Theory of Personality,* 1960) and Don D. Jackson ("The Question of Family Homeostasis," *Psychiatric Quarterly Supplement,* Pt. 1, Vol. xxxi, No. 1 [1957]:79–90), in "The Concept of the Family in Casework Theory," *Exploring the Base for Family Therapy,* edited by Nathan W. Ackerman, Frances L. Beatman, Sanford N. Sherman, p. 21 and note 19.

9. Sherman, *Exploring the Base,* 14, and note 2, traces attention to family roles to the 1944 work of Gomberg, "The Specific Nature of Family Casework," in *A Functional Framework to Family Casework* (University of Pennsylvania Press), 147.

10. Bradshaw, *Bradshaw On: The Family,* 39.

11. For a marvelous quick trip through what this would look like for parents and their children from infancy through adolescence, see "Parents and Children: For Each Other," in Donald M. Joy's *Bonding: Relationships in the Image of God* (Waco, TX: Word Books, 1985), 122–148.

12. Sandra D. Wilson, *Counseling Adult Children of Alcoholics,* Vol. 21 of Resources for Christian Counseling, Gary R. Collins, general editor (Dallas: Word Publishing, 1989), 54, citing the major research by Claudia Black, *It Will Never Happen to Me!* (Denver: M. A. C., 1982) and Sharon Wegscheider-Cruse, *Another Chance: Hope and Health for the Alcoholic Family* (Palo Alto: Science & Behavior Books, 1981).

13. Wilson, *Counseling Adult Children,* 54–58.

14. Joy, *Bonding,* 136–14

15. See, e.g., Bradshaw, *Bradshaw On: The Family*, 83, and Virginia Satir, *Peoplemaking* (Palo Alto, CA: Science and Behavior Books, 1972), ch. 13.

16. Ibid., 39. See Virginia Satir, *Peoplemaking* , ch. 7 on "The Rules You Live By." Satir identifies rules, along with self-worth, communication, and links to society as the four aspects of family life which she found continually "popping up in the troubled families" that came to her for help, *Peoplemaking*, 3.

17. "Family trance" is Bradshaw's powerful image in Bradshaw, *Bradshaw On: The Family*, 36–37.

18. Stephen Fleck, "Family Functioning and Family Pathology," *Psychiatric Annals* 10, no. 2, (February, 1980): 48, and Satir, *Peoplemaking*, ch. 5 and 6 on "Patterns of Communication" and "Communication Games."

19. The term is Satir's, *Peoplemaking*, with the book cover subtitle, "because you want to be a better parent."

20. Murray Bowen, *Family Therapy in Clinical Practice* (New York: Jason Aronson, 1978), 27, from an article previously published in 1959.

21. Fleck, 50–54. Building on the insights of Midelfort and others in the early 1950s regarding the family as a system, by 1960 Bowen had come to regard "schizophrenia as a process that requires three or more generations to develop," moving through successive stages to clinical impairment (*Family Therapy*, p. 51).

22. Such as in Bradshaw, *Bradshaw On: The Family*, Figure 4.1, p. 63.

23. Bradshaw, *Bradshaw On: The Family*.

24. Jane Middleton-Moz, *Children of Trauma: Rediscovering Your Discarded Self* (Deerfield Beach, FL: Health Communications, Inc., 1989), 98.

25. For full-length treatments of this concept, see John Bradshaw, *Healing the Shame that Binds You* (Deerfield Beach, FL: Health Communications, Inc., 1988), and Sandra D. Wilson, *Released from Shame: Recovery for Adult Children of Dysfunctional Families* (Downers Grove, IL: InterVarsity Press, 1990).

26. See Bradshaw, *Bradshaw On: The Family*, 69–72, 92–99; Wilson, *Released from Shame*, ch. 2, "Understanding Shame and Stumbling;" Middleton-Moz, *Children of Trauma*, 11, 35 ff., 140–152.

27. Middleton-Moz, *Children of Trauma*, 7, 23–25, 51–62.

28. Robert W. Firestone, with Joyce Catlett. *The Fantasy Bond: Effects of Psychological Defenses on Interpersonal Relations* (New York: Human Sciences Press, 1987), chap. 6.

29. Middleton-Moz demonstrated this in her studies of *Children of Trauma*. Her clients were not only children of the trauma of dysfunctional or abusive families, but children of holocaust survivors, families with catastrophic illness, immigrants with attendant cultural trauma, violence, cultural self-hate. She writes of "children of trauma" as children who "throughout their developmental years faced 'cumulative traumas' [such as emotional deprivation, war zone life, minority status, physical handicapping] . . . They might never remember what really happened, yet buried feelings and emotional reactions to these experiences may direct the course of their lives. As adults these individuals may suffer from panic attacks, bulimia, chronic depression, antisocial behavior, compulsive behavioral problems and addictions," 4. "Adult children of trauma often become locked in unhealthy and addictive relationships. These patterns reflect repeated survival attempts to master old pain," patterns like choosing not to have children, not bonding to their children, or becoming "over enmeshed or permissive," 4–5.

30. Janet Geringer Woititz, *Adult Children of Alcoholics* (Hollywood, FL: Health Communications, 1983), 3.

31. Woititz, *Adult Children*, 2.

32. Ibid., 4.

33. As far removed from Woititz' work as Sandra D. Wilson's evangelical presentation in Resources for Christian Counseling series, *Counseling Adult Children of Alcoholics*, 46–52, 58 ff. and David Seamands' widely read *Putting Away Childish Things* (Wheaton, IL: Victor Books, 1983). See also Bradshaw, *Bradshaw On: The Family*, 88–89.

34. Bradshaw, *Bradshaw On: The Family*, 88–89.

Chapter 5

1. On the causes of alcoholism see Wilson, *Counseling Adult Children*, 6–8, for a helpful review of the research (including her own doctoral work) as well as the first three chapters of *Alcoholism and Substance Abuse: Strategies for Clinical Intervention* (New York: The Free Press, 1985), edited by Thomas E. Bratter and Gary G. Forrest.

2. Joseph L. Kellermann, in *Al-Anon Faces Alcoholism*, 22.

3. William S. Sloan, in *Al-Anon Faces Alcoholism*, 45.

4. Bradshaw, *Bradshaw On: The Family*, 89, quoting the World Health Organization's definition. On extension of the concept of addiction, see *Bradshaw On: The Family*, 95. For approaches to this same conclusion from different perspectives, see Wilson, *Counseling Adult Children*, 141–142; Firestone, *The Fantasy Bond*, ch. 10, particularly 156 ff.; and Middleton-

Moz, *Children of Trauma*, 125, 130. Ms. Middleton-Moz treats compulsive, addictive behaviors (lists overeating, gambling, spending, workaholism, relationship addictions, bulimia, shoplifting, hoarding, anorexia) as "born from feelings of intense cravings for nurturing, affection and personal power," representing "the child's attempt at survival, security, satisfaction, identity and safety," 125.

5. Pia Mellody with Andrea Wells Miller and J. Keith Miller, *Facing Codependence: What it Is, Where it Comes from, How it Sabotages Our Lives* (San Francisco: Harper & Row, 1989), ix–xiii, xvi–xxiv. The appendix to this work provides extensive bibliography and a review of the literature on codependence. Similarly, see Firestone's treatment of the fantasy bond between couples and of the approach to life developed out of negative self-image in his *The Fantasy Bond*, chapters. 3, 7 and 8. For the history of the concept see *Co-Dependency, An Emerging Issue* (Hollywood, FL: Health Communications, 1984).

6. That is, they stayed in abusive relationships not because of well-thought-through religious convictions or conscious decisions to suffer as an expression of their devotion to Christ, but because they themselves could not surrender the relationship. Andrea Wells Miller and J. Keith Miller in *Facing Codependence*, xii.

7. Wilson, *Released from Shame*, 128. In *Counseling Adult Children* she contrasts codependency with the healthy capacity to be "interdependent," 77.

8. Bradshaw, *Bradshaw On: The Family*, 166.

9. Mellody, *Facing Codependence*, 4, and elaborated in succeeding chapters.

10. Adapting from Wilson, *Counseling Adult Children*, 79, who adapts Melody Beattie's nine-page lists of the distinguishing marks of codependents, *Codependent No More: How To Stop Controlling Others and Start Caring for Yourself* (New York: HarperCollins Publishers, 1987), 37–45.

11. Bradshaw, *Bradshaw On: The Family*, 209.

12. Wolin, Steven J., and Sybil Wolin, *The Resilient Self: How Survivors of Troubled Families Rise Above Adversity* (New York: Villard Press, 1993). The book reports findings from their own work with troubled families, and reports a growing literature on how persons cope successfully with adversity.

13. Ibid., 18.

14. Ibid., chapters 1, "The Challenge of the Troubled Family," and 2, "To Name the Damage Is to Conquer It," along with repeated returns to the absolute necessity of facing the damage head-on.

15. Ibid., 163.

16. Ibid., ch. 9, "Morality: Holiness in an Unholy World," 184–204.

Part 3

1. Jeffrey D. Imbach, *The Recovery of Love: Christian Mysticism and the Addictive Society* (New York: Crossroad, 1992), 21, 29.

2. C. F. Midelfort, *The Family in Psychotherapy* (New York: McGraw-Hill Book Company, 1957), 13 and 191.

Chapter 6

1. An interpretive translation. Andrew T. Lincoln, *Ephesians*, Vol. 42, Word Biblical Commentary (Dallas, TX: Word Books, Publisher, 1990), p. 300, translates to pseudos as "falsehood," but then argues on the basis of use and its tie with Colossians 3:8, 9 against taking it to mean "deception as a way of life." This seems to me to miss the breadth of the problem of falsehood implied in the context, 4:17–19, and also does not take seriously enough the programmatic nature of the teachings begun here.

2. The picture is Middleton-Moz's, *Children of Trauma*, 168.

3. Kenneth Collins notes boredom, anguish and insight from experience as tools which can expose "The Delusions of the Self," *Soul Care*, 99–102.

4. See Bradshaw, *Bradshaw On: The Family*, 39, 77, 83; Wilson, *Counseling Adult Children*, 54–58; Satir, *Peoplemaking*, ch. 13, for starters.

5. Satir, *Peoplemaking*, 98.

6. Ibid., 98–99, adapted from present to past tense expression.

7. Bradshaw, *Bradshaw On: The Family*, 63.

8. Mellody, *Facing Codependence*, 21–28

9. Seamands' book, *Putting Away Childish Things*, then exposes childhood mottoes which destroy, and the putting away of childish ideas of love and marriage, God and His will, prayer, childhood confusions, childish dependency on feelings, and childish concepts of self and self-surrender.

Chapter 7

1. Compare Lincoln, *Ephesians*, 301.

2. Firestone, *The Fantasy Bond*, 126–131.

3. Scott Peck, *The Road Less Traveled: A New Psychology of Love,*

Traditional Values and Spiritual Growth (New York: Simon and Schuster, 1978), 69–70.

4. Firestone, *The Fantasy Bond*, 87–99.

5. Satir, *Peoplemaking*, 101–102; the other critical issue determining family health, according to Ms. Satir, concerns attitudes toward affection and sex.

6. Firestone, *The Fantasy Bond*, 129.

7. Question exists as to whether the exhortation in v. 27 to give no place to the Devil should be paired with the sayings on anger in v. 26 or should stand on its own. Its general content rather comes "out of the blue" in the series of other instructions aimed at specific behavioral or attitudinal matters, and thus supports its attachment to v. 26. The parallel connection of anger with the Devil in the pseudoepigraphic work, *The Testament of Daniel*, 4:7–5:1, also supports the connection (cited by Lincoln, *Ephesians*, 302).

8. Wilson's expression, *Counseling Adult Children*, 137.

9. Lyman C. Wynne, "The Study of Intrafamilial Alignments and Splits in Exploratory Family Therapy," in *Exploring the Base for Family Therapy*, eds. Nathan W. Ackerman, et. al., (New York: Family Service Association, 1961), 110.

10. Bradshaw, *Bradshaw On: The Family*, 53–54, with adaptation in some cases from gerund to imperative (e.g., "being" to "be"). Cf. David Augsburger's helpful *Caring Enough to Confront*.

11. Wilson, *Counseling Adult Children*, 259.

12. As we know from his awareness of the teachings of Jesus on such speific topics as divorce and sexual practice (1 Cor.7:12–20) and table fellowship with non-Jews (Gal. 2:11–14).

13. See David Hagner, *The Jewish Reclamation of Jesus* (Grand Rapids: Eerdmans, 1984), 105–112, for more insight on the issues involved in such paragraphs.

14. NRSV, "He took them up in his arms." The word "enfolded" is more beautiful than "took up in his arms." "Embraced them," "enfolded them in his arms," "wrapped them up in his arms" would really catch it better.

Chapter 8

1. Lincoln, *Ephesians*, 303, sets aside this approach to the participle with article here, noting that in such constructions the articular present participle "virtually becomes a noun and has a timeless force." Too much

must not be made of these things, of course. Still, it remains true that a perfectly fine noun for "thief" was easily at hand, a term Paul uses in 1 Corinthians 6:10 ("neither thieves . . ." AOT). Even as a virtual noun, the participle still names by characteristic behavior, and brings that to the forefront more than the simple noun could.

2. Various cultures expect and allow different distances, but each has such a "space."

3. Mellody, *Facing Codependence*, 11.

4. Ibid., adapting from singular to plural.

5. Ibid., 11. See also Sandra Wilson's discussion of personal boundaries in her treatment of "major issues of codependency," *Counseling Adult Children*, 181.

6. Middleton-Moz, *Children of Trauma*, 35. See her whole treatment on the boundary loss from parenting to meet the parents' needs, 29–36.

7. Wilson, *Released from Shame*, 74.

8. Garth Wood, *The Myth of Neurosis: Overcoming the Illness Excuse* (New York: Harper & Row, 1983), 152–155.

9. Scott Peck, *People of the Lie: The Hope for Healing Human Evil* (New York: Simon & Schuster, 1983), 84 and 118.

10. Peck, *The Road Less Traveled*, 15–18.

11. Pelagius, a chief protagonist of St. Augustine in the early fifth century, denied humans inherit any sin from Adam and claimed all humans now have power not to sin. Humans are not bound in sin, but have simply followed Adam's bad example. Hence, "Pelagianism," a viewpoint rejected by the church.

12. Mellody, *Facing Codependence*, 4 and ch. 2.

13. Ibid., 28–34.

14. Ibid., 29–30.

15. Wilson, *Counseling Adult Children*, 104, who names "identifying feelings" and "problem solving" as the other two.

16. Ibid., 116.

17. Melody Beattie, *Codependent No More* (San Francisco: HarperCollins Publishers, 1987), 200–201.

18. Wilson, *Counseling Adult Children*, 77.

19. Nathan W. Ackerman, *Treating the Troubled Family* (New York: Basic Books, 1966), 72.

20. Mellody, *Facing Codependence*, 13–21.

21. Ibid., 14.

22. Collins emphasizes this effectively in his chapters, "The Construction of the Kingdom of Self;" "The Enslavement of the Self;" "The Self Threatened;" and "The Delusions of Self," *Soul Care*, 32–119.

Chapter 9

1. Satir, *Peoplemaking*, 30. Satir's pioneering writing on communication is regarded as among the most insightful in the entire recovery literature.

2. The adjective used means literally something "decayed, rotten," like fish (Matt. 13:48) and fruit (Matt. 12:33). By extension it is used to describe things that are unsound or "bad, evil, unwholesome," as here (W. Bauer, *A Greek-English Lexicon of the New Testament and Other Early Christian Literature*, eds. W. F. Arndt and F. W. Gingrich; 2nd revised edition, F. W. Gingrich and F. W. Danker [Chicago: University of Chicago Press, 1979), 749.

3. Mellody, *Facing Codependence*, chapters 10–14. See pages 156 ff., 171–172.

4. Ibid., 170–171.

5. Most of these communication blocks and some of the examples are from Michael H. Popkin's *Active Parenting of Teens: Parents Guide* (Atlanta, GA: Active Parenting, Inc., 1990), 108–114. John Gottman's study of thousands of marriages shows how much of "marriage style" turns out to be "communication style." Gottman's chapter on "The Four Horsemen of the Apocalypse: Warning Signs" reveals what these speech modes do to a marriage. See his *Why Marriages Succeed or Fail* (New York: Simon & Schuster, 1994), 68–102.

6. Bradshaw, *Bradshaw On: The Family*, 51–52, 80–82.

7. Satir, *Peoplemaking*, 79.

8. Satir, *Peoplemaking*, 72–78; quote from 72–73. For the skeptics she adds, "And lest leveling seems too unrealistic to you, let me assure you that you can still placate if you choose, blame if you like, be on a head trip, or be distracting. The difference is you know what you are doing and are prepared to take the consequences for it." See John Gottman's "Marriage Styles: The Good, the Bad, and the Volatile" in his *Why Marriages Succeed or Fail*, 32–67.

9. Mellody, *Facing Codependence*, 21–28.

10. This paragraph follows Pia Mellody's outline in *Facing Codependence*, 21.

11. Bradshaw, *Bradshaw On: The Family*, 50.

Chapter 10

1. "all malice." My translation follows NEB, "bad feeling of every kind."

2. Lincoln, *Ephesians*, 309 (cf. Romans 1:29).

3. Bradshaw, *Bradshaw On: The Family*, 95.

4. Ibid., 94–95.

5. Wilson, *Counseling Adult Children*, 73.

6. Firestone, *The Fantasy Bond*, 309.

7. Bradshaw, *Bradshaw On: The Family*, 70.

8. Ibid., 132.

9. Ibid., 130.

10. *Firestone, The Fantasy Bond*, 294.

11. James and Phyllis Alsdurf, *Battered Into Submission: The Tragedy of Wife Abuse in the Christian Home.* (Downers Grove, IL: InterVarsity Press, 1989), chapter two.

12. Whatever the "submission" of wives to their husbands finally means for contemporary families, it cannot mean the right of anyone, including a husband, to "rule" and abuse his wife.

13. Alsdurf and Alsdurf, *Battered Into Submission*, Chapter 3, "What Kind of Men Abuse Their Wives?" and the studies cited there.

14. Alsdurf and Alsdurf, *Battered Into Submission*, pp. 42–43.

15. *The Violence Within* (New York: Harper & Row, 1978), p. 10, cited in *Battered*, p. 41.

16. Daniel Jay Sonkin and Michael Durphy, *Learning to Live Without Violence: A Handbook for Men* (CA: Volcano Press, 1989, updated).

17. In words like this "passive voice" means the subject of the verb is acted upon: "I was hit by the ball;" "active voice" means the subject is doing the acting: "I hit the ball."

18. Wilson, *Released from Shame*, 167.

19. Wilson, *Counseling Adult Children*, 133, citing Freil and Freil, *Adult Children: The Secrets.*

20. Wilson, *Counseling Adult Children*, 133.

21. Bradshaw, *Bradshaw On: The Family*, 145.

22. Wilson, *Counseling Adult Children*, 120.

23. Alsdurf and Alsdurf, *Counseling Adult Children*, 143–148.

24. Following Wilson, *Released from Shame*, 122–124, with some adaptation.

25. Alsdurf and Alsdurf, *Battered*, 105, with reference to Anne Rood, "Looking the Snake in the Eye," *Jubilee*, January 1996, p.1.

26. "Of this gospel I have *become* a servant," 3:7; "*Become* kind, tenderhearted . . ." 4:32; "*Become* imitators of God," 5:1; "That it might *go* well for you," 6:3. "*Be* partakers," 5:7 and "*Be* wise," 5:17 show examples that do not appear to denote process; 5:12 denotes happening, as may 6:3.

27. Lyman C. Wynne, "The Study of Intrafamilial Alignments and Splits in Exploratory Family Therapy," in *Exploring the Base for Family Therapy*, eds. Nathan W. Ackerman, et. al., (New York: Family Service Association, 1961), 108–109.

28. Alsdurf and Alsdurf, *Battered*, 106.

29. Wilson, *Released from Shame*, 169–171.

Chapter 11

1. Christian discipleship here parts company significantly with "spiritualities" of the Mormon Church and the New Age movement—the former polytheistic, the latter pantheistic.

2. See my study, "The Godly and the Good Life in Biblical Thought," for more extended discussion of this: *Christian Scholar's Review*, XXII:3 (1993): 248–266. Even the confidence of some of the church's own saints—that God's love pervades the universe and may be experienced directly in the experience of that universe—stands open to biblical critique at this point. Cf. Jeffrey D. Imbach, *The Recovery of Love: Christian Mysticism and the Addictive Society*, parts II & III, on Julian of Norwich and John Russbroec. For more on the idea of a "canonical conversation," see my *Bible Study That Works* (Nappanee, IN: Evangel Press, 1994), 65–84.

3. Recall Firestone's conclusions about the pervasive presence of primal pain, *The Fantasy Bond*, 294, and Wilson's graph of family functioning, *Counseling Adult Children*, 17–18.

4. Wilson, *Counseling Adult Children*, 95–99. Cf. her *Released from Shame*, 149–151.

5. Curt Cloninger, *God-Views*. Word LifeWare Video. (Waco, TX: Word, 1985).

6. Joy, *Bonding*, chapters one, two and nine. Without accepting Dr. Joy's understanding of the sexually undifferentiated "Alpha Adam," which he sees created in Genesis 2 (pp. 14–17), one still gains immense

profit from the many evidences he is able to marshal to demonstrate that *"Basic human intimacies are images of the most profound spiritual reality* [the reality of God-human relationships]; they are God's 'first curriculum'" (176–177).

7. C. F. Midelfort, *The Family in Psychotherapy* (New York: McGraw-Hill Book Company, 1957), 12–13.

8. "Marasmus" is a disease of whole-person atrophy afflicting severely love-deprived children.

9. Lloyd H. Ahlem, *Do I Have to Be Me? Living with Myself and Liking It* (Ventura, CA: Regal Books, 1973), chapters one and two; quote from page 25. This "little" book has 176 pages of small print, information-jammed material.

10. See Wolfhart Pannenberg, "Feminine Language About God?" *The Asbury Theological Journal*, 48, No. 2 (Fall, 1993): 27–30. Malachi 2:10–12 may be an exception to this.

11. Cf. Elizabeth Achtemeier's excellent article, "Why God Is not Mother," *Christianity Today* (August 16, 1993):16–23.

12. Bradshaw, *Bradshaw On: The Family*, 94.

13. Firestone, *The Fantasy Bond*, 101–113.

14. Wilson, *Counseling Adult Children*, 152.

15. Ahlem, *Do I Have to Be Me?*, chapters 7 and 14. Cf. Sandra Wilson's discussion of the need for a power higher than oneself and one's parents to which to give oneself authentically, in *Counseling Adult Children*, 92.

16. Bradshaw, *Bradshaw On: The Family*, 172.

Chapter 12

1. Tim Stafford, "The Hidden Gospel of the 12 Steps," *Christianity Today* 35, no. 8 (July 22, 1991):16.

2. As John Wesley, the founder of Methodism, repeatedly emphasized and as writers from widely differing perspectives claim in their discussions of human personal and moral development.

3. For example, John Bradshaw, *Creating Love* (New York: Bantam Books, 1992). Outside the recovery movement one thinks immediately of Scott Peck's analysis in *The Road Less Traveled* of essential human personal formation as growth in love.

4. Books like *Five Views on Sanctification* (Grand Rapids: Academie Books/Zondervan Publishing House, 1987) and *Christian Spirituality* (edited by Donald L. Alexander; Downers Grove, IL: InterVarsity Press,

1988) show this. See particularly the various responses to Wesleyan Melvin E. Dieter's presentation in *Five Views on Sanctification*, pp. 47–57. See J. I. Packer's outstanding *Rediscovering Holiness* (Ann Arbor, MI: Servant Publications, 1992) for a non-Wesleyan exposition of Christian holiness and pages 110–112 for his main quarrel with "second blessing" understandings of this experience.

Works Cited

Achtemeier, Elizabeth. "Why God Is not Mother," *Christianity Today* (August 16, 1993):16–23.

Ackerman, Nathan W. *Treating the Troubled Family.* New York: Basic Books, 1966.

Ackerman, Nathan W., Frances L. Beatman, and Sanford N. Sherman. *Exploring the Base for Family Therapy.* New York: Family Service Association, 1961.

Ahlem, Lloyd H. *Do I Have to Be Me? Living with Myself and Liking It.* Ventura, CA: Regal Books, 1973.

Al-Anon Faces Alcoholism. New York: Al-Anon Family Group Headquarters, Inc., 1965.

Alcoholics Anonymous: The Story of How Many Thousands of Men and Women Have Recovered from Alcoholism. New York City: Alcoholics Anonymous Publishing, 1954; first published in 1939.

Alsdurf, James and Phyllis Alsdurf. *Battered Into Submission: The Tragedy of Wife Abuse in the Christian Home.* Downers Grove, IL: InterVarsity Press, 1989.

Arndt, W. F. and F. W. Gingrich. *A Greek-English Lexicon of the New Testament and Other Early Christian Literature.* Second edition, rev. and augmented by F. W. Gingrich and F. W. Danker. Chicago: University of Chicago Press, 1979.

Beattie, Melody. *Codependent No More: How to Stop Controlling Others and Start Caring for Yourself.* New York: HarperCollins Publishers, 1987.

Bowen, Murray. *Family Therapy in Clinical Practice.* New York: Jason Aronson, 1978.

Bradshaw, John. *Bradshaw On: The Family, a Revolutionary Way of Self-Discovery.* Deerfield Beach, FL: Health Communications, 1988.

_____. *Healing the Shame that Binds You.* Deerfield Beach, FL: Health Communications, Inc., 1988.

Bratter, Thomas E. and Gary G. Forrest (eds.). *Alcoholism and Substance Abuse: Strategies for Clinical Intervention.* New York: The Free Press, 1985.

Buechner, Frederick. *Telling Secrets.* San Francisco: Harper & Row, 1989.

Cloninger, Curt. *God-Views.* Word LifeWare Video. Waco, TX: Word, 1985.

Collins, Kenneth J. *Soul Care: Deliverance and Renewal Through the Christian Life.* Wheaton, IL: Victor Books, 1995.

Firestone, Robert W. with Joyce Catlett. *The Fantasy Bond: Effects of Psychological Defenses on Interpersonal Relations.* New York: Human Sciences Press, 1987.

Fleck, Stephen. "Family Functioning and Family Pathology," *Psychiatric Annals* 10, no. 2, (February, 1980): 48–54.

Gottman, John. *Why Marriages Succeed or Fail.* New York: Simon & Schuster, 1994.

Guirguis, Waguish R. "The Family and Schizophrenia," *Psychiatric Annals* 10, no. 7 (July, 1980): 269–275.

Hagner, David. *The Jewish Reclamation of Jesus.* Grand Rapids: Eerdmans, 1984.

Howells, John G. "An Overview of Family Psychiatry," *Psychiatric Annals* 10, no. 2 (February, 1980): 40–45.

Imbach, Jeffrey D. *The Recovery of Love: Christian Mysticism and the Addictive Society.* New York: Crossroad, 1992.

Joy, Donald M. *Bonding: Relationships in the Image of God.* Waco, TX: Word Books, 1985.

Lincoln, Andrew T. *Ephesians.* Vol. 42, Word Biblical Commentary. Dallas, TX: Word Books, Publisher, 1990.

Mellody, Pia with Andrea Wells Miller and J. Keith Miller. *Facing Codependence: What it Is, Where it Comes from, How it Sabotages Our Lives.* San Francisco: Harper & Row, 1989.

Middleton-Moz, Jane. *Children of Trauma: Rediscovering Your Discarded Self.* Deerfield Beach, FL: Health Communications, Inc., 1989.

Midelfort, C. F. *The Family in Psychotherapy.* New York: McGraw-Hill Book Company, 1957.

New Revised Standard Version Bible. National Council of the Churches of Christ in the United States of America, 1989.

Pannenberg, Wolfhart. "Feminine Language About God?" *The Asbury Theological Journal*, 48, No. 2 (Fall, 1993): 27–30.

Peck, Scott. *People of the Lie: The Hope for Healing Human Evil.* New York: Simon & Schuster, 1983.

_____. *The Road Less Traveled: A New Psychology of Love, Traditional Values and Spiritual Growth.* New York: Simon and Schuster, 1978.

Popkin, Michael H. *Active Parenting of Teens: Parents Guide.* Atlanta, GA: Active Parenting, Inc., 1990.

Satir, Virginia. *Peoplemaking.* Palo Alto, CA: Science and Behavior Books, 1972.

Seamands, David. *Putting Away Childish Things.* Wheaton, IL: Victor Books, 1983.

Sonkin, Daniel Jay and Michael Durphy. *Learning to Live Without Violence: A Handbook for Men.* CA: Volcano Press, 1989, updated.

Stafford, Tim. "The Hidden Gospel of the 12 Steps," *Christianity Today* 35, no. 8 (July 22, 1991): 14–19.

_____. "The Therapeutic Revolution," *Christianity Today* 37, no. 6 (May 17, 1993): 24–32.

Thompson, David L. "The Godly and the Good Life in Biblical Thought," for more extended discussion of this: *Christian Scholar's Review*, XXII:3 (1993): 248–266.

_____. *Bible Study That Works.* Nappanee, IN: Evangel Press, 1994.

Wilson, Sandra D. *Counseling Adult Children of Alcoholics*, Vol. 21 of Resources for Christian Counseling, Gary R. Collins, general editor. Dallas: Word Publishing, 1989.

_____. *Released from Shame: Recovery for Adult Children of Dysfunctional Families.* Downers Grove, IL: InterVarsity Press, 1990.

Woititz, Janet Geringer. *Adult Children of Alcoholics.* Hollywood, FL: Health Communications, 1983.

Wolin, Steven J., and Sybil Wolin, *The Resilient Self: How Survivors of Troubled Families Rise Above Adversity.* New York: Villard Press, 1993.

Wood, Garth. *The Myth of Neurosis: Overcoming the Illness Excuse.* New York: Harper & Row, 1983.